LANGSTON HUGHES

Recent Titles in Greenwood Biographies

J.K. Rowling: A Biography
Connie Ann Kirk

The Dalai Lama: A Biography
Patricia Cronin Marcello

Margaret Mead: A Biography
Mary Bowman-Kruhm

J.R.R. Tolkien: A Biography
Leslie Ellen Jones

Colin Powell: A Biography
Richard Steins

Pope John Paul II: A Biography
Meg Greene Malvasi

Al Capone: A Biography
Luciano Iorizzo

George S. Patton: A Biography
David A. Smith

Gloria Steinem: A Biography
Patricia Cronin Marcello

Billy Graham: A Biography
Roger Bruns

Emily Dickinson: A Biography
Connie Ann Kirk

LANGSTON HUGHES

A Biography

Laurie F. Leach

GREENWOOD BIOGRAPHIES

GREENWOOD PRESS
WESTPORT, CONNECTICUT · LONDON

Library of Congress Cataloging-in-Publication Data

Leach, Laurie F.
  Langston Hughes : a biography / Laurie F. Leach.
    p. cm—(Greenwood biographies, ISSN 1540–4900)
  Includes bibliographical references and index.
  ISBN 0–313–32497–2 (alk. paper)
  1. Hughes, Langston, 1902–1967. 2. Poets, American—20th century—Biography. 3. African American poets—Biography. 4. African Americans in literature. I. Title. II. Series.
PS3515.U274Z676 2004
818'.5209—dc22
[B]   2003060131

British Library Cataloguing in Publication Data is available.

Library of Congress Catalog Card Number: 2003060131
ISBN: 0–313–32497–2
ISSN: 1540–4900

First published in 2004

Greenwood Press, 88 Post Road West, Westport, CT 06881
An imprint of Greenwood Publishing Group, Inc.
www.greenwood.com

Printed in the United States of America

∞

The paper used in this book complies with the Permanent Paper Standard issued by the National Information Standards Organization (Z39.48–1984).

10 9 8 7 6 5 4 3 2 1

Copyright Acknowledgments

The author and publisher gratefully acknowledge permission to reprint the following:

Excerpts from *The Collected Poems of Langston Hughes* by Langston Hughes, copyright © 1994 by The Estate of Langston Hughes. Used by permission of Alfred A. Knopf, a division of Random House, Inc. in the world excluding the British Commonwealth. Reprinted by permission of Harold Ober Associates, Incorporated in the British Commonwealth.

Quotations from various letters and other unpublished writings of Langston Hughes reprinted by permission of Harold Ober Associates, Incorporated.

From ARNA BONTEMPS—LANGSTON HUGHES LETTERS 1925-1967: six short extracts. Copyright © 1980 by George Houston Bass, executor and trustee u/w Langston Hughes. Reprinted by permission of Harold Ober Associates, Incorporated.

From *Life of Langston Hughes:* four short extracts. Copyright © 1986, 1988 by The Estate of Langston Hughes.

Photographs of Hughes from the Yale Collection of American Literature, Beinecke Rare Book and Manuscript Library, reprinted with permission of Harold Ober Associates, Incorporated.

For my colleagues and students at Hawai'i Pacific University

CONTENTS

Photo essay follows page 76

SERIES FOREWORD

In response to high school and public library needs, Greenwood developed this distinguished series of full-length biographies specifically for student use. Prepared by field experts and professionals, these engaging biographies are tailored for high school students who need challenging yet accessible biographies. Ideal for secondary school assignments, the length, format, and subject areas are designed to meet educators' requirements and students' interests.

Greenwood offers an extensive selection of biographies spanning all curriculum related subject areas including social studies, the sciences, literature and the arts, history and politics, as well as popular culture, covering public figures and famous personalities from all time periods and backgrounds, both historic and contemporary, who have made an impact on American and/or world culture. Greenwood biographies were chosen based on comprehensive feedback from librarians and educators. Consideration was given to both curriculum relevance and inherent interest. The result is an intriguing mix of the well known and the unexpected, the saints and sinners from long-ago history and contemporary pop culture. Readers will find a wide array of subject choices from fascinating crime figures like Al Capone to inspiring pioneers like Margaret Mead, from the greatest minds of our time like Stephen Hawking to the most amazing success stories of our day like J.K. Rowling.

While the emphasis is on fact, not glorification, the books are meant to be fun to read. Each volume provides in-depth information about the subject's life from birth through childhood, the teen years, and adulthood. A thorough account relates family background and education, traces personal and professional influences, and explores struggles, accomplishments, and contributions. A timeline highlights the most significant life events against a historical perspective. Bibliographies supplement the reference value of each volume.

ACKNOWLEDGMENTS

The research and writing of this book was supported by three grants from the Trustees' Scholarly Endeavors Program of Hawai'i Pacific University. I am especially grateful for two course releases that enabled me to pursue this project.

I would like to thank several of my colleagues for their contributions, support, and encouragement, especially Deborah Ross who connected me with Greenwood Press in the first place; Phyllis Frus, who gave me the push I needed to get my proposal done in time to qualify for a course release in the fall of 2002; Catherine Sustana, Jacqueline Langley, and Marlena Bremseth for friendly interest and encouragement; and Skip Kazarian, Micheline Soong, Houston Wood, and Patrice Wilson for volunteering to be my first readers and making helpful suggestions on my draft. I was also able to present a portion of this research at HPU's Faculty Scholarship Day in August 2002, and I thank all who attended and offered comments and suggestions.

I am indebted to Taran Schindler of the Beinecke Rare Book and Manuscript Library for assistance in obtaining copies of documents in the Hughes archive in the James Weldon Johnson collection. Craig Tenney of Harold Ober Associates helped me to obtain the necessary permissions from the Langston Hughes Estate and Alfred A. Knopf.

This book could not have been written without the research and scholarship of many others. For the facts and chronology of Hughes's life, I have drawn primarily on Arnold Rampersad's acclaimed two-volume biography, *The Life of Langston Hughes*, published by Oxford University Press in 1982 and 1986 and republished in a paperback edition with new afterwords in February 2002 to commemorate the poet's centennial. My debt to Rampersad's exhaustive archival research is attested in my citations of correspondence and other unpublished materials as quoted by Rampersad. An earlier biography by Faith Berry, *Langston Hughes: Before and Beyond Harlem* (Lawrence Hill, 1983), offered me a number of interesting insights and details. The research of these two scholars was invaluable in determining when to trust Hughes's own autobiographical works, *The Big Sea*, and *I Wonder as I Wander* as sources for this biography. A very important source for understanding and reconstructing the *Mule Bone* controversy was the 1991 Harper Perennial edition of the play by George Houston Bass and Henry Louis Gates, Jr., which reprints various correspondence from participants in the controversy. Christopher De Santis's *Langston Hughes and the* Chicago Defender (University of Illinois, 1995) provided access to many of Hughes's important newspaper columns and was instrumental to my writing of the chapter on Hughes and the Freedom Movement.

Finally I would like to thank my husband, Tak-Sang Cheng, and daughters, Crescent and Sophie, for their love, encouragement, and the gift of both time apart so I could finish this book and, more importantly, time together.

INTRODUCTION

Langston Hughes was the most prominent African American poet of the twentieth century, a leading figure in the Harlem Renaissance, and an outspoken critic of racism and segregationist policies. In his poetry he strove to speak to, as well as for, the black masses while still making a living from his writing, which meant attracting white audiences, as well. One of his major innovations was to incorporate the African American vernacular and cultural traditions, including the rhythms of black music, into his poetry. Although the lecture circuit wearied him, he connected easily with live audiences and often read his works to the accompaniment of black musicians and singers.

He may be best known as a poet, but he worked in nearly every literary genre and was the author of two novels, two autobiographies, more than thirty stage plays, several opera librettos, and three collections of short stories, in addition to the five collections of stories and newspaper columns featuring the character of Jesse B. Semple. In addition to writing the "Simple" columns, Hughes used his weekly column in the *Chicago Defender* to speak out on social issues, especially to condemn Jim Crow policies and to protest the anti-communist hysteria of McCarthy and others. He was also a translator, an anthologist, and the author of many children's books.

In both his youth and again in his later years, Hughes traveled widely, forging connections between American blacks and Africans and representing the culture and concerns of African Americans to the world. At the time of his youthful travels, especially in the Soviet Union and in Spain at the time of the Spanish Civil War, he was also a journalist, recording his observations for readers at home. In his later years, he was a cultural ambassador who often witnessed performances of his own works in the countries he visited.

After his early poems made him one of the stars of the Harlem Renaissance, Hughes earned a degree at Lincoln University and produced a second book of poems and his first novel, *Not Without Laughter*. After much emotional trauma, Hughes broke free of the demands of a controlling and possessive patron and quarreled with Zora Neale Hurston over the authorship of a play they had worked on together. A liberating trip to Cuba and Haiti, his first reading tour of the South, and the Scottsboro case all contributed to Hughes's radicalization. Hughes traveled, lived, and worked in the Soviet Union in the early 1930s and then settled in California where he continued to write radical verse and plays with socialist themes. Hughes eventually distanced himself from the left in the 1940s, but he never disavowed his admiration for the Soviet Union's efforts to eliminate racism. During World War II he strove to connect the fight against fascism to the struggle against Jim Crow. When the war ended with segregation still in place, he noted the incompleteness of this victory for African Americans. Hughes contributed to the civil rights struggle for the rest of his life by continuing to speak out against segregation in his columns, plays, and poetry. He had just completed work on *The Panther and the Lash*, a collection of "poems for our time" dedicated to one of the heroes of the civil rights movement, when he died in 1967.

His proudest achievement, as he indicated during his acceptance of the Spingarn Medal for 1960, was that he was the first black American whose work was permeated with racial consciousness to make his living as a writer. His medal, said Hughes, could only be accepted in the name of his fellow blacks who were both his inspiration and his devoted audience.

The focus of this book is biography; although I have tried to relate the life to the works and to give readers an account of the themes and significance of Hughes's writing, there has not been space for extensive literary criticism nor for quotation of Hughes's poetry. For all poems mentioned, I have given a page reference to the *The Collected Poems of Langston Hughes* so that the interested reader can easily look up and read the poem while reading the biography. Hughes's poetry is also available in a three-volume edition published in 2001, as volumes 1–3 of the University of Missouri edition of the *Complete Works of Langston Hughes*.

In keeping with contemporary preferences I have used the words "black" or "African American" where Hughes would likely have used "Negro" or "colored."

TIMELINE

1902	James Langston Hughes born in Joplin, Missouri, on February 1. Later that year, his father relocates to Mexico.
1907	Brief reunion in Mexico between James Hughes and his wife, son, and mother-in-law.
1908	Begins school in Topeka, Kansas, where he is living with his mother. Parents divorce at some point between 1907 and 1914.
1908–1915	Lives primarily in Lawrence, Kansas, with his grandmother while his mother travels looking for work. At times stays with his mother in other cities.
1915	Mother marries Homer Clark who has a two-year-old son. Grandmother dies and a few months later he is left behind with family friends while the Clarks move to Lincoln, Illinois. He joins them there that summer.
1916	Moves to Cleveland and enrolls in Central High School.
1918	Spends a summer in Chicago.
1919	Visits his father in Mexico during the summer.
1920	Graduates from Central High School. Composes "The Negro Speaks of Rivers." Moves to Mexico to live with his father.
1921	"The Negro Speaks of Rivers" published in the *Crisis*. Enrolls at Columbia. Makes first contacts in Harlem.
1922	Drops out after one year at Columbia. Father suffers a stroke. Works on mother ship. Writes many of the poems that would appear in his first book. Befriends Countee Cullen and corresponds with Alain Locke.

1923	Sails to Africa and Rotterdam as a messman. Continues to publish with the help of Cullen. In August the *Crisis* devotes a whole page to his poems.
1924	Sails to Europe, heading for Paris. Works on jazz- and blues-inspired poems, has romance with Anne Coussey, and is visited by Alain Locke. Returns to New York in November and meets Arna Bontemps and Carl Van Vechten.
1925	Lives with his mother and stepbrother in Washington, D.C. *Survey Graphic* issue on Harlem published. Wins first prize in *Opportunity* contest. Knopf accepts his first book of poetry for publication. "Discovered" as busboy poet by Vachel Lindsay.
1926	Hughes attends Lincoln University with financial support from Amy Spingarn. Publishes *The Weary Blues*.
1927	Writes "The Negro Artist and the Racial Mountain." Publishes *Fine Clothes to the Jew*. Introduced to Mrs. Mason (Godmother) in April, tours the South in the summer, begins formal patronage arrangement in November.
1928	At Godmother's urging, begins to write first novel, *Not Without Laughter*.
1929	Graduates from Lincoln. Revises novel. Visits Cuba.
1930	Works on play *Mule Bone* with Zora Neale Hurston. Publishes *Not Without Laughter*. Serves as dramatist-in-residence at Hedgerow Players. Writes *Mulatto* (play).
1931	Quarrels with Hurston over authorship of *Mule Bone*. Wins Harmon Award. Visits Haiti. Makes reading tour of the South. Publishes *Dear Lovely Death* and *The Negro Mother and Other Dramatic Recitations*.
1932	Publishes *The Dream Keeper* and *Scottsboro Limited: Four Poems and a Play*. With Bontemps publishes *Popo and Fifina*. Travels to Moscow to work on a Soviet film that is never made. Tours Soviet Asia. Writes socialist verse including poem "Goodbye Christ."
1933	Lives in Moscow. Begins writing short stories again. Has brief romance with Sylvia Chen. Visits Japan, Korea, Shanghai, and Hawaii. Lives in Carmel-by-the Sea, California.
1934	Publishes *The Ways of White Folks*. Writes *Blood on the Fields* with Ella Winter. Member of the John Reed Club. In July, flees Carmel for San Francisco after receiving threats. Attacked in the local press as a Communist agitator. Father dies. Travels to Mexico to settle father's affairs.

1935   Returns to California. YMCA cancels speaking engagement
            due to protests. Visits mother in Ohio. Martin Jones brings
            version of *Mulatto* to Broadway. Writes "Let America Be
            America Again." Writes the play *Little Ham* for Gilpin Play-
            ers in Cleveland. Mother diagnosed with cancer. Wins
            Guggenheim grant to work on novel set in Chicago.

1936   Moves to Chicago to research his novel. Writes *When the
            Jack Hollers* with Bontemps. Writes *Angelo Herndon Jones*,
            which wins *New Theatre* magazine contest. Begins working
            on a nonmusical version of his unfinished opera about Haiti,
            Troubled Island. Pursued romantically by Elsie Roxborough.

1937   *Drums of Haiti* staged in Detroit. *Joy to My Soul* staged at
            Karamu House. Goes to California to work on *Troubled Is-
            land* with William Grant Still. Speaks at the Second Inter-
            national Writers Congress in Paris and covers the Spanish
            Civil War for the *Baltimore African American* and other pa-
            pers. In November returns to Harlem. Establishes Harlem
            Suitcase Theater.

1938   Makes a lecture tour for International Workers Order,
            which publishes *A New Song* (collection of socialist verse).
            Don't You Want to Be Free? premieres at Harlem Suitcase
            Theater in April. Mother dies in June. Attends conference
            in Paris. Writes *The Organizer, Young Man of Harlem, Front
            Porch.* Rowena Jelliffe rewrites third act of *Front Porch* and
            Gilpin Players perform the play.

1939   Makes a cross-country lecture tour with Bontemps, then re-
            mains in California to work on film scripts for *God Sends
            Sunday* and *Way Down South.* Speaks at Third American
            Writers Conference in New York. In Chicago and Califor-
            nia, writes *The Big Sea.* Resigns as director of Harlem Suit-
            case Theater.

1940   Completes a long lecture tour. Works for American Negro
            Exposition in Chicago. Moves to Los Angeles to write lyrics
            for a "Negro Revue" with the Hollywood Theater Alliance.
            Publishes *The Big Sea.* Picketed by followers of Aimee Sem-
            ple MacPherson. Repudiates "Goodbye Christ."

1941   Hospitalized in California. Recuperates in Carmel. Sells his
            books to Knopf for $400. Writes *Shakespeare in Harlem.* Wins
            Rosenwald Fund grant. In November moves to Chicago and
            founds the Skyloft Players and works on the musical *The Sun
            Do Move.* Returns to Harlem and lives with the Harpers.

1942   Publishes *Shakespeare in Harlem*. Joins Writers' War Committee Advisory Board, writes radio scripts and war-bond jingles. Writes lyrics for popular songs with several collaborators. *Sun Do Move* premieres in April. Spends summer at Yaddo. Begins writing a weekly column for the *Chicago Defender*.

1943   Creates the character of Jesse B. Semple who frequently appears in his *Defender* columns. Exempted from the draft. Publishes *Jim Crow's Last Stand*. Frequently publishes essays in *Common Ground*. Encounters pickets on a reading tour. Receives an honorary doctorate from Lincoln University. As riots break out across the United States, participates in radio programs aimed at calming racial tensions in New York.

1944   Attacks segregation on radio program, *America's Town Meeting of the Air*. Begins major speaking tour with Feakins, Inc. speakers bureau. Repurchases the rights to his first five books from Knopf. Embarks on a tour of high schools, sponsored by Common Council for American Unity. Tour proceeds with the Council's support despite attacks on Hughes.

1945   War ends. Makes second speaking tour with Feakins. Removed from FBI's list of suspected Communists for lack of evidence of significant activity. Turns to assembling a collection of apolitical "lyric" poetry, *Fields of Wonder*. Begins working with Elmer Rice and Kurt Weill on *Street Scene*.

1946   Hughes continues to work on *Street Scene*. Converts Simple columns into a book but cannot find a publisher.

1947   *Fields of Wonder* published. Hughes teaches creative writing at Atlanta University. *Street Scene* successful on Broadway, earning Hughes substantial royalties. William Grant Still withdraws *Troubled Island* from the City Center and unsuccessfully tries to interest the Metropolitan Opera in it. Hughes writes *One-Way Ticket* and works on anthology of Negro poetry with Bontemps. Composer Jan Meyerowitz proposes a collaboration to make an opera based on the short story "Father and Son." Hughes visits Jamaica.

1948   Hughes driven from lecture circuit by increasingly strident protests about his alleged Communist sympathies and anti-Christian writings. City Center once again prepares to stage *Troubled Island*. Dispute with Still over splitting royalties for the lyrics with Vera Avery, Still's wife. Purchases his own home in Harlem and lives there with the Harpers for the rest of his life. Publishes anthology with Bontemps, *Poetry of the Negro 1746–1949*.

1949   Teaches at University of Chicago's Laboratory School. *Troubled Island* premieres. Works on the lyrics for *Just Around the Corner*. Publishes *One-Way Ticket*.

1950   *The Barrier* successfully produced at Columbia University. Publishes *Simple Speaks His Mind*. *Just Around the Corner* plays in a summer theater in Maine but is not brought to Broadway. *The Barrier* comes to Broadway and closes after three shows.

1951   Makes a brief reading tour of the South. Denounced in *Red Channels: A Report of the Communist Influence in Radio and Television*. Publishes *Montage of a Dream Deferred*.

1952   Publishes *Laughing to Keep from Crying*. Protests derail a reading tour. Publishes *The First Book of Negroes*.

1953   Appears before the Senate Permanent Sub-Committee on Investigations. Publishes *Simple Takes a Wife* which wins Anisfield-Wolf Book Award in Race Relations. Begins converting the story into a play, *Simply Heavenly*.

1954   Publishes *The First Book of Rhythms* and *Famous American Negroes*. Publishes five more children's books in the next six years.

1955   Rewrites *Simply Heavenly* as a musical. With Roy De Carava publishes *The Sweet Flypaper of Life*. Works on his autobiography.

1956   Focuses 3rd collection, *Simple Stakes a Claim*, on civil rights issues. Publishes *I Wonder as I Wander*. With Milton Meltzer publishes *A Pictorial History of the Negro in America*. Writes *Tambourines to Glory* as a gospel play, then converts it into a novel.

1957   Edits *Book of Negro Humor* with Bontemps. *Esther* (opera with Meyerowitz) premieres. *Simply Heavenly* produced by Stella Holt. Translates Gabriela Mistral's poetry.

1958   *Langston Hughes Reader* and *Selected Poems of Gabriela Mistral* published. *Tambourines to Glory* (novel) published. *Simply Heavenly* produced in London. *Book of Negro Folklore* published.

1959   Publishes *Selected Poems*. Lectures in Trinidad. Works on anthology of African writing.

1960   Wins Spingarn Medal. Writes *Ask Your Mama*. Publishes *An African Treasury*. *Port Town* (opera with Meyerowitz) premieres. *Tambourines for Glory* plays in Connecticut. Travels to Nigeria and Paris.

1961   Accepted to the National Institute of Arts and Letters. Begins writing history of NAACP. Publishes *Ask Your Mama*. Writes *Black Nativity* and *The Prodigal Son*. *Black Nativity* premieres on Broadway in December. Hughes travels to Nigeria for a cultural festival.

1962   Begins column for the *New York Post*. Visits Uganda and Ghana. Publishes *Fight for Freedom*. Participates in National Poetry Festival in Washington, D.C. *Black Nativity* tours Europe. *The Gospel Glory* premieres.

1963   Publishes *Something in Common*. Writes *Jericho-Jim Crow*. Receives honorary doctorate from Howard University. Takes European tour. *Tambourines to Glory* premieres.

1964   *Jericho-Jim Crow* premieres. Edits the *Book of Negro Humor*. Attends Berlin Folk Festival where *Black Nativity* is performed.

1965   Participates in State Department-sponsored European tour. *Prodigal Son* premieres. Works on the script of *The Strollin' Twenties*. *Prodigal Son* tours Europe. Publishes *Simple's Uncle Sam*.

1966   Discontinues columns about Simple. *The Strollin' Twenties* produced on television. Publishes *The Book of Negro Humor*. Makes a reading tour of Africa after attending the First World Festival of Negro Arts in Dakar. Works with Bontemps on revision of *Poetry of the Negro*. Publishes *The Best Short Stories by Negro Writers*.

1967   Dies on May 22. *The Panther and the Lash* is published posthumously.

Chapter 1

LONELY BOY

Born in cold and darkness, near midnight in the midst of a Missouri winter, Langston Hughes would find much of his childhood equally bereft of light and warmth. His mother, Carrie, would often leave him in the care of his grandmother while she lived and worked in other cities. As for his father, we do not know whether James Nathaniel Hughes returned from Cuba to Joplin, Missouri, for the birth of his son on February 1, 1902, but we do know that he lived apart from his wife for much of her pregnancy, and that he moved alone to Mexico to work as a secretary to an executive of an American-owned company before the boy was nine months old. Though the child was named James Langston Hughes, his family called him simply "Langston" and a potential link with his absent father was quietly erased.

James Hughes had married Carolina Mercer Langston on April 30, 1899, in Guthrie, Oklahoma, where she had been working as a schoolteacher. He had come to Oklahoma territory as a homesteader, after studying law in Kansas and previously working as a law clerk, schoolteacher, and surveyor's assistant. James Hughes was not allowed to sit for the bar in Oklahoma due to his race, and soon after the marriage, he found a job in Joplin as a stenographer for a mining company.

Carrie and James were ill matched in temperament and the marriage was apparently an unhappy one. Their firstborn son was either stillborn or died shortly after birth and was buried without being given a name on February 8, 1900. The couple moved to Buffalo, New York, in March 1901, and in September, Carrie returned home in mid-pregnancy while James pursued his plans to move to Cuba.

Langston's parents did make one attempt at reconciliation. In the spring of 1907, when Langston was five, his mother traveled with him and his maternal grandmother to meet his father in Mexico, where he had settled. The reunion was short-lived, for a frightening earthquake on April 14, 1907, caused the trio to flee. Though James continued to send Carrie money to help support his son, there was no further personal contact, and eventually, in circumstances that remain indistinct, the couple divorced.

Carrie was bitter about the failure of her marriage, and perhaps more so about her straitened financial circumstances and her inability to realize her dream of a career in theater. Sometimes she would turn her anger on young Langston, telling him that he was just like his father whom she described as "a devil on wheels" and "as mean and evil a Negro as ever lived" (BS 36). At other times she indulged him with trips to the theater. Often she left him in Lawrence, Kansas, in the care of her mother while she traveled and looked for work in places such as Colorado Springs, Kansas City, or Topeka.

Carrie's mother, Mary Sampson Patterson Leary Langston, was approaching 70 years when Langston first came to live with her. Langston remembered her as a proud, elderly woman who seldom went out and expressed little emotion. However, she did like to take Langston on her lap and tell him about the greatness of his ancestors.

As a free woman of African, Indian, and French heritage living in North Carolina, Mary Patterson had been vulnerable to attempts by whites to enslave her, and so in 1857 at approximately age 21 she moved north to Oberlin, Ohio. Enrolled in the preparatory program of the university there, she met and married an abolitionist, Lewis Sheridan Leary, whose racial background was similar to her own. After their marriage in 1858, they both served as conductors on the Underground Railroad, helping fugitive slaves escape to the North. Leary participated in the raid on the arsenal at Harper's Ferry led by radical abolitionist John Brown. Shot in the aftermath of the raid, Leary died of his wounds, and his widow treasured the shawl, bloody and rent by bullets, that he was wearing when he died. She sometimes wore the shawl and used it to cover her grandson at night.

Mary remarried 10 years later to another abolitionist, Charles Howard Langston, who had been a friend of Lewis Leary. Charles's father was a white planter named Ralph Quarles, who chose to live with Lucy Langston, a former slave, as if they were husband and wife. At his death, Quarles left his money and property to his three sons by Lucy: Gideon, Charles, and John Mercer Langston. All three attended Oberlin and supported the cause of abolition. Though Charles was too old to fight in the Civil War, he served the Union cause as a recruiter. Unable to establish a successful political career after the war, Charles nevertheless remained prominent in the black community in Lawrence. His younger brother, John Mercer Langston, was even more successful, building a career in both politics and higher education that culminated in the presidency of a Virginia college and service in the U.S. Congress as a representative from Virginia.

Langston Hughes's early poem, "Aunt Sue's Stories," is drawn from his experience of hearing his grandmother's tales about his ancestors. Like "the dark-faced child" of the poem, young Langston listened attentively, knowing that these tales of slavery and heroism were "real stories." He came to feel that he had to live up to a proud tradition by doing something himself to serve and uplift the race (CP 23–24).

In some ways, though, Langston was an outsider to much of the black community in Lawrence. As Rampersad points out, although Lawrence had been founded by abolitionists in 1854, it was becoming an increasingly segregated community by the end of the nineteenth century. Restaurants, hotels, and even churches that had once admitted both blacks and whites were now closed to black patrons. While a few long-term black settlers, such as the Langstons, lived in neighborhoods that were predominantly white, most of the black population either lived in North Lawrence or in the "Bottoms" in extreme poverty (LLH I: 8). Langston was intrigued by the glimpses he caught of this world during the times he and his grandmother lived in the home of James and Mary Reed because Mary Hughes had rented her home to university students. The Reeds were friends of the family whom Langston came to regard as aunt and uncle. Unlike his grandmother, who had stopped going to church in a protest against segregation, Mary Reed took him not only to her own church, St. Luke's Methodist Episcopal Church, but over to the decidedly less genteel Warren Street Baptist Church where Langston was entranced by the sights and sounds of Southern black religious fervor. He also enjoyed the speeches and theatricals put on as part of the forum sponsored by the church on Sunday afternoons.

At school, too, he was sometimes set apart from other black students. He began school in 1908 in Topeka, where he had been temporarily reunited with his mother. Carrie successfully appealed to the school board to allow Langston to attend the Harrison Street School, which was more convenient to her residence but which otherwise had only white pupils, rather than the distant school for Negro children located on the other side of the railroad tracks. However, the boy was harassed by his teacher, who seated him in a back corner, and by some of his classmates, although others befriended him. In one specific incident that Langston long remembered, his teacher confiscated some licorice from one of his classmates. She warned him against eating the black candies: "They'll make you black like Langston. You don't want to be black, do you?" (qtd. in *LLH* I:13).

Back in Lawrence he attended the Pickney School, which had segregated classrooms in the lower grades, but he later switched to integrated schools that had few black students. Though Langston did consistently well in his studies, in seventh grade he again had to contend with a racist teacher. When the teacher forced all the black children to sit together in a separate row, Langston made up cards that said JIM CROW ROW and placed them on each desk in the row. When the teacher moved to reprimand him, he ran out of the classroom, yelling that his teacher had a Jim Crow row. Though Hughes was expelled, he was allowed to return to school after protests by several black parents.

In March 1915, Langston's grandmother Mary died. Carrie arrived for the funeral accompanied by a new family. Sometime earlier his mother had married Homer Clark, who had a two-year-old son, Gwyn Shannon Clark (nicknamed "Kit"), by an earlier marriage. Briefly, the three Clarks lived with Langston in his grandmother's house, but when Homer left to find work, Carrie and Kit soon followed. Langston was left with the Reeds to finish his seventh-grade year.

During those final months in Lawrence, Langston had a disillusioning experience with religion that he later described in *The Big Sea*. Mary Reed's church had been sponsoring a revival and she had been bringing Langston along in the expectation that he would be saved. She had told him that as part of the conversion experience he would see a light and feel Jesus in his soul. Langston took her literally and waited expectantly on the mourners' bench for the moment when Jesus would call him. Finally, when only he was left on the bench, Langston gave in to the congregation's expectations and pretended to be saved. Miserably conscious of his hypocrisy, and realizing that he had lost his faith since Jesus had ignored his sincere appeal, Langston cried in his bed that night. His grief was only compounded when his Aunt Reed mistook his tears for joy at being saved, and he could not bear to tell her the truth.

By age 13 then, Langston Hughes felt abandoned by his father, who was still in far-off Mexico; his grandmother, who had died; his mother, who had left with her new husband and adopted son; and now, Jesus. Perhaps these early experiences of isolation and rejection led Hughes to hold himself aloof later in life, avoiding intimate relationships for fear of being abandoned. Certainly they fostered in him a fierce independence that contributed to strained relationships with those who later sought to influence and control him, including both his parents and his first patron.

Chapter 2

CLASS POET

In the summer of 1915, after finishing his seventh-grade year, Langston Hughes took the train from Lawrence, Kansas, to Lincoln, Illinois, to join his mother, his stepfather, Homer Clark, and his adopted brother, Gwyn "Kit" Clark. In the fall he enrolled in the eighth grade at Central School, where he and a female classmate were the only black students. Langston seemed to adjust well to his new surroundings, excelling in his school-work, making new friends, acquiring a part-time job, and being elected class poet.

Hughes wrote self-deprecatingly of this honor in *The Big Sea*, claiming that the position of class poet was left over after all the other class officers had been elected. Since no one in the class had written a poem, his class-mates chose him out of benign racial prejudice, believing all Negroes to possess an innate sense of rhythm. Hughes claimed that his poetic career began with the writing of the 16-verse graduation poem—later shortened for delivery—that lavishly praised his teachers and the graduating class and was greeted with thunderous applause (*BS* 24).

Hughes's account of how he first came to think of himself as a poet or even a writer at all is probably overly modest. As Rampersad points out, his teachers at Central School viewed him as an outstanding student, and Ethel Welch, whom Hughes remembered as his favorite teacher, would later recall him as one of the three best writers in her English classes that year (*LLH* I: 24). Whether or not his eighth-grade classmates knew of his writing talent when they chose him as class poet, surely his high school classmates did when they conveyed the same honor on him four years later.

But this honor took place in a different city. Homer Clark missed his stepson's graduation because he had gone to look for work in Cleveland; Carrie, Langston, and Kit joined him there at the end of the summer, in time for Langston to start high school at Cleveland's Central High. Once again, Hughes was one of a few black students in a largely white student body, composed primarily of children of immigrants. The school had high academic standards and Langston plunged eagerly into its life. He ran on the track team, wrote for the school newspaper and the literary supplement *The Belfry Owl,* and in his senior year edited the yearbook as well. He befriended a Polish Catholic boy, Sartur Adrezejewski, and several Jewish students, noting that as a Negro he was one of the few to bridge the religious divides among members of the student body (*BS* 30).

It was good that Hughes found such a congenial environment at school, for the city itself was not so welcoming, nor was his home life easy. For example, he struggled to find a summer job, for many business owners had a policy against hiring blacks. Cleveland at this time was adjusting to a large influx of African Americans drawn to work in the city's manufacturing industries. Since the city was segregated, this meant overcrowding and high rents for the growing black population, and Hughes recalled that throughout his time in high school, he or his family paid high rents for a series of attic or basement apartments (*BS* 27).

In fact Langston was only to live with his family for about a year before Homer moved on. Homer had found work as a machinist in a steel mill, putting in long hours and bringing home good wages, but the work was grueling. At some time during his high school years, Langston wrote a poem about the steel mills that both "grind out steel / And grind away the lives of men" ("Steel Mills," *CP* 43). Homer suffered under the intense heat of the mills and, like the workers in the poem, was turning into an "old man" before his time. He quit his job and found another as a janitor, but Carrie was forced to go to work as a maid to make up for the lost income, leaving little Kit with a hired babysitter. Tension between Homer and Carrie grew until Homer left for Chicago. Within a few months Carrie followed him, and Hughes moved out of the basement apartment in which his family had lived and into an attic room where he lived alone, feeding himself on rice and hot dogs, except for those times when he would join the Adrezejewski family for a meal. Although he visited his mother and stepbrother in Chicago in the summer of 1918—Homer had once more left them behind—he did not enjoy the experience, which included a beating by a gang of white boys who resented his having intruded into their neighborhood. The congestion in the black areas was even worse than in Cleveland, and Langston chose to return to Ohio for his junior year.

According to Faith Berry, he made this choice over his mother's objections. Berry cites a passage in Hughes's second autobiography, *I Wonder as I Wander*, in which he describes arguing with his mother who expected him to quit school and go to work to help support her whenever his stepfather was not around (Berry 17; *IW* 308). Hughes would later use a fictional version of this conflict to close his novel *Not Without Laughter*. There, the narrator (Sandy) and his young aunt (Harriet) resist the demand of his mother (Anjee) that he continue with his summer job as an elevator operator rather than finish high school. Harriet convinces Anjee to let Sandy remain in school so that he might one day "help the whole race" rather than be "stuck in an elevator for ever" (323). Hughes would have versions of this quarrel with his mother for many years to come.

In Cleveland, Hughes formed an important friendship with a young couple, Russell and Rowena Jelliffe. The Jelliffes, who were white, were working to establish a community center for the inner-city residents of Cleveland. They established "Playground House" where Hughes was hired as one of the first teachers, giving art lessons to the neighborhood children.

Though he had already submitted several pieces to the school newspaper the previous year, including a variety of poems and some satirical prose, it was in the fall of 1918 that he became an editor. Although he claims in *The Big Sea* to have written only poetry (34), he actually wrote at least three short stories during his high school years, two of which were published in the *Central Monthly* during his junior year. Some of his poetry reflected the influence of his reading of poets such as Walt Whitman, Carl Sandberg, and Paul Laurence Dunbar in his high school English classes.

An unexpected letter from his father arrived in the late spring of 1919 inviting, or rather, commanding the presence of Langston in Mexico for the summer. Langston was eager to go, though a bit nervous, but he had to cope with his mother's outspoken resentment. She accused Langston of wanting to abandon her, after she had worked so hard to raise him, and told him she had been counting on him to help support the family by working over the summer.

Langston refused to give in to the pressure to stay, but the reunion got off to a bad start when, because of a misdirected telegram, he failed to meet his father's train. Once he located his father the next day, Langston was allowed only a half an hour to pack his bags and say good-bye to his furious mother. If his mother was too bitter to bid him a loving good-bye, his father was too distant to express any gladness at seeing him again after so many years. In this strained atmosphere, Langston solemnly accompanied his father on a journey toward Mexico and what he would describe in *The Big Sea* as the most "miserable" summer of his life (39).

On the trip south it soon became apparent that James Hughes and his son Langston were worlds apart in temperament and attitude. The father spoke disparagingly of both blacks and Mexicans, blaming them for their poverty and their exploitation at the hands of whites. James Hughes, in Langston's view, despised his own black skin. He had left the United States in order to escape the prejudice and racism that blocked his way to financial success. He had become both a successful lawyer and business-man in Mexico, where he was now the general manager of an American-owned company, Sultepec Electric Power and Light, as well as the owner of a ranch in Temexcaltepic. Smug in his achievements, he had only con-tempt for other blacks who continued to live in a country that doomed them to menial jobs, no matter their skills or education. Chief among these was Langston's mother, whom James had found working as a wait-ress. James emphasized that to avoid a similar fate, Langston must leave the United States permanently upon high school graduation.

Langston's father brought him to his house in the small valley town of Toluca, about 60 miles from Mexico City. Langston was appalled by his fa-ther's stinginess, and puzzled that he seemed to care so much for making money but refused to spend it, even for his own and his son's comfort. Langston provoked his father's rage by ordering good food from the local shops while James was away at the ranch and inwardly criticized his fa-ther's unwillingness to let his housekeeper's children share their meals or to provide his personal servant with a bed. There were no other English speakers around, and James worked long hours and traveled frequently, leaving Langston alone. Angry over his departure for Mexico against her wishes, his mother did not write to him. Out of boredom, Langston began to learn Spanish, and, at his father's insistence, bookkeeping and typing. But he often made mistakes in his figures only to be berated by his father for being unable to add at the age of 17.

Toward the end of the summer, however, James began to hold out the promise of a trip to Mexico City, where Langston could see the bullfights. But in the days preceding the trip his father was harsher than usual, always telling Langston to hurry and criticizing his progress in learning typing and bookkeeping. Langston seethed inwardly but did not protest. Finally on the morning they were to depart, James Hughes woke Langston at 4:30 and began shouting at him to hurry with his breakfast as he gulped down his own food. Langston was overwhelmed by nausea, dizziness, and anger. He got up from the table wordlessly and went back to bed, and his father left without him.

Even with his father gone, Langston could not bring himself to eat. When his father returned after four days, he sent him to the American hospital in Mexico City where Langston was three weeks recuperating. The physical manifestations of his illness included a high fever, intense nausea, and a lowered red blood cell count (*LLH* I: 34), but Hughes saw his experience as largely psychosomatic. As he explains in *The Big Sea*, he wanted to strike out at his father but could not. This illness was both a manifestation of his hatred for his father and a way of refusing to do what his father wanted, escaping from his control and costing him money at the same time (48–49).

Back in Cleveland, Langston enjoyed a busy and successful senior year at Central High, made even better by the fact that his father began sending him an allowance. The allowance and a part-time job enabled him to appease his mother by helping with the family expenses. Hughes added drama to his already long list of extracurricular activities including student council, track, French club, yearbook, and of course, the newspaper and literary magazine.

Hughes continued to write poetry and to share some of it with Rowena Jelliffe of Playground House. One memorable poem he wrote at this time was "When Sue Wears Red," a poem inspired by the sight of a young woman he had met at a school dance wearing a red dress. In the poem, he links the beauty of "Susanna" to that of an Egyptian queen and uses a refrain reminiscent of the passionate responses of the congregation in some of the black churches he had attended in childhood (*CP* 30). The poem represents one of his first attempts to write about a black subject from a black perspective.

Rowena Jelliffe's encouragement must have been important to Langston, for Carrie was impatient with his plans to write poetry or even to continue his education. Now that he was graduating from high school, she firmly expected him to go to work and start supporting her. Langston's desire to escape from these demands prompted him to accept his father's invitation to return to Mexico, despite the disaster of the previous summer and the real antipathy he now felt for his father. He hoped to convince his father to finance his education at Columbia, where the more affluent of his classmates from Central had been admitted. The fact that Columbia was adjacent to Harlem added to the attraction.

It was on his journey to Mexico that Langston would compose one of his greatest poems, "The Negro Speaks of Rivers" (*CP* 23):

I've known rivers:
I've known rivers ancient as the world and older than the
    flow of human blood in human veins.
My soul has grown deep like the rivers.

I bathed in the Euphrates when dawns were young.
I built my hut near the Congo and it lulled me to sleep.
I looked upon the Nile and raised the pyramids above it.
I heard the singing of the Mississippi when Abe Lincoln
        went down to New Orleans, and I've seen its muddy
        bosom turn all golden in the sunset.
I've known rivers:
Ancient, dusky rivers.
My soul has grown deep like the rivers.

The idea for the poem came to him as he looked out the window as the train crossed the Mississippi and began thinking of that river and its association with slavery. On the one hand, one of the worst fates that could befall a slave was to be "sold down the river" to the large slave market in New Orleans, sent away from his family to be worked to death on a cotton plantation. But the poem also invokes the legend that Abraham Lincoln witnessed a slave auction in New Orleans as a young man and resolved at that moment to overthrow slavery. The other rivers in the poem, such as the Congo and the Nile, also have connotations of slavery and exploitation by colonial powers but, like the Mississippi, are described in positive images. The speaker has bathed in the Euphrates, been lulled to sleep by the Congo, and seen the glory of a sunset on the Mississippi. The rivers are comforting, maternal presences, and the poem evokes a history of suffering, endurance, survival, and achievement.

Hughes demonstrates a masterful use of assonance in the long "o" sounds that echo through the poem in words like *known, older, flow, soul, grown,* and *golden* and employs a repetitive structure that gives the poem the solemn beauty of a litany. The poem also showed Hughes's embrace of and identification with the black race. He speaks in that poem not as Langston Hughes but as "The Negro." He embraces what his father rejected and disparaged, and now he would have to ask his father to support him in his endeavors.

His father, however, was not impressed. He ridiculed the idea that his son could support himself as a writer, especially a Negro writer. Furthermore, he was impatient with any idea that Langston seek his future in the United States, given the prevalence of the color line. His own plan was for his son to go to Switzerland or Germany, study engineering, then come back to work for him in Mexico. Langston was at least as horrified by this proposal as his father was by Langston's plans, and for the moment, the question of his future was left undecided. But Hughes was in effect trapped in Mexico, since James saw no reason to provide funds for him to return.

Although Langston was still unhappy living with his father, in many ways this yearlong visit was much more agreeable than his stay of the previous summer. His father had a new German housekeeper, Frau Schultz, who was a good cook and convinced his father to run a less Spartan household. Langston's Spanish improved and he was able to read books and make friends more easily. Most important, no matter what his father's opinion, Langston had decided to be a writer, and his time in Mexico gave him hours to write. Hughes sent poems to the *Brownies' Book* a magazine for black children founded by W. E. B. DuBois, and the editor, Jessie Fauset accepted some of the poems and asked for more. In January, Hughes sent her "The Negro Speaks of Rivers" and Fauset accepted it for the *Crisis,* DuBois's adult literary magazine for which she was also literary editor.

In the fall, Hughes found a way to earn money as an English teacher. He taught classes at a private school in the morning and a business college in the afternoon and also took on several private pupils. He began to save his money towards his return fare to New York; he was determined to see Harlem even if he could not afford college.

A disturbing incident took place in the spring of 1921. During the previous winter after the brewmaster's wife had died, Frau Schultz had arranged for Gerta Kraus, the teenaged daughter of one of her friends from Mexico City, to take the job of housekeeper for the widower. Gerta managed well but she was lonely, for she spoke no Spanish and the brewmaster was old and short-tempered. Gerta came frequently in the afternoons for coffee and conversation with Frau Schultz. Langston, not understanding German, usually kept to another part of the house and barely knew Gerta. That spring, Gerta's mother came to visit from Mexico City and spent the week with Frau Schulz. Accordingly, Gerta came to the house for several hours each afternoon. The brewmaster, who had fallen in love with Gerta, became convinced that she was spending so many hours at the Hughes household because she was having an affair with Langston. On the last day of Frau Kraus's visit, he came to the house in a rage, brandishing a gun. The German women were there alone. He shot Gerta three times and also fired on Frau Schultz. Unable to find Langston on the property, he turned himself into the police and was eventually sentenced to 20 years. Fortunately, both women survived, but Hughes was shaken.

This tragic and violent incident combined with two others—a streetcar accident which severed the legs of an Indian peasant and a Mexican girl's suicide-by-drowning in a shallow fountain—to make Langston eager to leave Mexico. He continued to save his money from teaching. He also continued to write and submit work to Jessie Fauset including poems, children's stories, and essays about life in Mexico. When "The Negro

Speaks of Rivers" appeared in the June 1921 issue, Langston showed the magazine to his father as proof of his literary potential. James was dismissive when he learned that his son had not been paid for his contributions, but nevertheless agreed to finance one year at Columbia. Langston applied from Mexico and was accepted, and in September took a boat from Vera Cruz to Manhattan.

Chapter 3

THE LURE OF HARLEM

Arriving in Manhattan on September 4, 1921, Langston Hughes felt he had arrived in the city of his dreams. What he most longed to see was Harlem and other black faces; so after spending an expensive night in a hotel in Times Square, he headed for the Harlem branch of the YMCA at 181 West 135th Street, where he rented a fourth-floor room for $7 a week.

Harlem at this time was beginning to be referred to as "the Negro City." Until 1905, no African Americans had lived in Harlem; by 1921, whites were an uneasy minority. Like other northern cities, New York attracted many black migrants from the South in the early twentieth century, and the majority of them had settled in Harlem. Although, as in Cleveland, the large houses in which whites had formerly lived were being subdivided into smaller apartments that rented for more than the entire house had previously commanded, the quality of the housing was relatively good, and Harlem was viewed as a desirable neighborhood for an up-and-coming young black person.

Harlem was fast becoming the cultural center of black America. Magazines like the *Crisis* (where Hughes's poem "The Negro Speaks of Rivers" had just been published), and the *Messenger* (a socialist magazine) were headquartered there. Plays featuring black casts and themes had recently been successful on Broadway.

Thrilled to be in Harlem at last, Hughes was somewhat reluctant to leave his room at the YMCA for a dorm room at Columbia, nor was the housing office eager to accept him. Roughly 12 black students had been admitted to Columbia that year, but none was permitted to live in the dormitories. Hughes's reservation, made from Mexico, had been accepted

because the housing department had not realized his race. When he arrived to check in, he was told that all the rooms had already been reserved. But since Hughes could prove that his deposit had been accepted,
he was grudgingly allowed to occupy a room on the first floor of Hartley
Hall.

That hurdle over, Hughes faced another embarrassing problem. The tuition that his father was supposed to have wired to New York by the start
of the semester had not arrived. When Hughes telegraphed his father, he
was told the money had already been mailed, and Columbia granted an
extension until October 5. But the money still did not come. Hughes repeatedly telegraphed his father and applied for postponement of his bills.
He was able to borrow some money from company officers in the New
York office of the light company for which his father worked in Mexico,
and he finally received $532 from his father in November. The delayed
funds were blamed on misdirected mail, but it was not an auspicious beginning to Langston's college career.

Langston and his father continued to quarrel over money. As the winter set in, Hughes found his wardrobe inadequate and wrote requesting
money for long underwear and an overcoat, but his father did not immediately reply. When he did send $300 for the next semester, it was accom-
panied by complaints about his son's grades and a warning that there
would not be further money forthcoming. (He had earned mostly Bs, with
one C in French, but had dropped physics to avoid failing it.) When
Hughes indignantly replied that the $300 was insufficient, and that wor-
ries about finances took time away from his studies, his father challenged
him to justify his expenditures (qtd. in *LLH* I: 54). In *The Big Sea*, Hughes
contends that part of the problem was that he was also giving part of his
allowance to his mother, something he may have wished to conceal from
his father (84). In any case, he was offended by his father's demand that
he account for all his expenditures, foreshadowing the problems he would
later have with his patron. In a letter to his father written in March 1922,
Langston enclosed the requested statement but not without a tone of
wounded innocence. Did his father believe he was wasting his allowance
or worse, deceiving him about his expenses? Langston protested again
that having to watch every penny made it impossible for him to concentrate on his studies, as would supplementing his income with a job. Perhaps already having made up his mind to leave Columbia at the end of the
year, he told his father that he would rather have no support than be badg-
ered in this way (qtd. in *LLH* I: 55).

Financial troubles and quarrels with his father were not all that challenged Langston during his year at Columbia. Even though he had bro-

ken the color line by living in the dormitory, he found it hard to mingle socially with his fellow students. His only close friend was a Chinese student named Yee Sing Chun. The white students froze him out of their organizations, even the school newspaper. The editorial staff of the *Spectator* discouraged him while pretending to give him a chance by assigning him to report the fraternity news for his "try-out" piece (*BS* 83). He did publish four poems in the April and May issues of the *Spectator* under the pseudonym Lang-Hu. As Faith Berry remarks, this pen name sounds like "Lang Who?" reflecting "the way Hughes felt as a Columbia student—unsure, unknown and unwelcome" (29). Furthermore, the school seemed too large and impersonal, and Langston felt little interest in the subjects he was studying.

A poem he wrote much later in life, while not strictly autobiographical, may capture some of his feelings of disconnection and isolation. In "Theme for English B," a 22-year-old enrolled at Columbia who is "the only colored student in [his] class," contemplates an assignment to write a personal essay. The speaker walks down the steps from the school and into Harlem in order to write his assigned page, insisting that while he has much in common with the instructor and the other students, his living in Harlem, his being "colored," and his love for African American culture, represented by "Bessie and bop" are essential parts of his identity, despite not being valued or understood by the dominant culture, represented by the instructor. Hughes's speaker notes that the black and white traditions are both part of American culture but that neither is always comfortable acknowledging this coexistence and interdependence. Langston's attendance at Columbia was partly an attempt to disprove James Hughes's thesis that America would never allow a black man to advance socially, intellectually, and economically. Langston would demonstrate that he did not need to go abroad to be educated or become financially successful, but could do so in his own country. But his experience of the rigid color line at Columbia had been a discouraging reminder that "you [white America] don't want to be a part of me." What may have been more important for Hughes at this point, however, was the opposing realization that "nor do I often want to be a part of you." While the poem closes by affirming the relationship and that the two, instructor and student, white and black, learn from each other, Langston felt an irresistible pull away from the "college on the hill" to the steps that "lead down into Harlem" (*CP* 409–10).

Whenever he could, Hughes visited Harlem. Jessie Fauset, learning that he was at Columbia, invited him to the *Crisis* office, where she was editor, to meet and have lunch with DuBois. He also met Augustus

Granville Dill, who was the business manager at the *Crisis* and who invited Hughes to spend the Christmas vacation at his apartment. Throughout the year Langston attended lectures and readings at the Harlem Branch Library and wrote poems about black people and Harlem life. He continued to publish in the *Crisis*, but even though he bought his father a subscription to the magazine, James Hughes did not praise his son's successes there.

In May, Hughes received word from one of his father's colleagues, R.J.M. Danley, that his father was seriously ill in Mexico, having suffered a stroke. He sent a message of regret but declined to go visit when Danley's son arrived from Mexico with $100 from Langston's father. Upon further inquiry from the senior Danley, Langston explained that given the strained relationship he and his father shared, he did not feel a visit would be helpful. If the $100 were intended to fund his travel to Mexico, he would instead return it. He also indicated that he had decided to leave Columbia (qtd. in *LLH* I: 57).

Although his father's health gradually improved, the stroke cost James the use of his right arm. He did not answer the letters in which Langston repeated his refusal to go to Toluca and his lack of interest in returning to Columbia. At one point, Langston contemplated taking classes as an extension student; but when the fall came, he did not attend, and eventually he returned the $100 to his father.

After finishing his exams in May, Langston found a room in a Harlem boarding house. He struggled to find a job, for most advertised positions were not open to black applicants. Finally he found work on a vegetable farm on Staten Island for the duration of the summer and for which he received $50 a month plus room and board. At the end of the summer, he made a brief visit to McKeesport, Pennsylvania, where Homer, Carrie, and Kit had settled. Returning to Manhattan, he took a job delivering flowers for a Fifth Avenue florist, but was fired for coming late to work after about a month. As he looked for work again, he began to think of going to sea and in October secured a job as a messman, a server in the ship's dining room, without realizing that he would be working on one of the mother ships anchored at Jones Point. These ships housed the men who tended to the surplus fleet owned by the U.S. Shipping Board. Hughes had become a crewman on a ship that would not leave port.

Initially disappointed that he would not get a chance to travel as he had hoped, Hughes grew to enjoy the job. The sailors were friendly; there were many books in the ships' libraries, and there was ample time to write. He continued to correspond with Jessie Fauset and send her his work. She encouraged him even though she disapproved of his dropping out of Columbia, but as a messman, Hughes stopped receiving invitations to lunch with the Harlem elite.

A friendship he had formed the previous year with Countee Cullen, a 20-year-old poet he met at the Harlem Branch Library, blossomed during this time. Hughes stayed with Cullen whenever he visited Manhattan. Cullen and he, though writing in very different styles, shared their work with each other. Cullen watched for the appearance of Hughes's poems in the *Amsterdam News* and sent along clippings. However, Hughes did not show Cullen the greatest poem he produced during this time, "The Weary Blues," a poem in which he strove to capture in poetry the spirit and rhythm of the blues (*CP* 50). Hughes's work was also beginning to be noticed by the whites who were interested in "Negro literature." Some of his poems were chosen by Robert T. Kerlin, a white university professor, for his anthology *Negro Poets and Their Poems*.

Cullen urged his older friend and mentor, Alain Leroy Locke, to write to Hughes, and soon Hughes and Locke were exchanging warm letters. Locke was a former Rhodes scholar and a Harvard graduate, who was a professor at Howard University. Locke pressed for an invitation to visit Hughes, but Hughes put him off, claiming that he worried about being too "stupid" to make a good first impression. Interested in cultivating the careers of young black writers, Locke suggested forming a coterie of writers comprising Cullen, Jean Toomer (who was about to publish *Cane),* and Hughes. In an early letter to Locke acquainting him with his past history, Hughes spoke of the excitement of spending the previous year in New York and voiced his desire to see the great European cities (qtd. in *LLH* I: 67). Locke responded with news of his plans to travel in Europe that summer and urged Hughes to join him, but Hughes ultimately declined, injuring Locke's feelings.

Hughes was ready to travel but unwilling to commit himself to be Locke's companion. Both Locke and Cullen were homosexuals, and Hughes perhaps sensed, but refused to acknowledge directly, the romantic undercurrent to Locke's letters. According to Rampersad, Cullen, working to retain his friendship with both men, tried to soothe Locke's feelings by explaining that Langston had not understood Locke's discreet professions of interest (*LLH* I: 71).

Hughes, meanwhile, began to search for a ship that would take him abroad. Though disappointed to lose at the last moment a berth on a ship bound for Constantinople, in June he found a position on the *West Hesseltine*, a freighter bound for Africa.

Chapter 4

AT SEA

The *West Hesseltine* was due to sail from New York on June 13, 1923, leaving 21-year-old Langston only two days to get ready. As he prepared for his voyage to Africa, he thought to retrieve a box of books he had left with someone in Harlem during his year at Jones Point. Hughes brought the books aboard with him, but when he opened the box the first night, near Sandy Hook, New Jersey, they reminded him not only of his misery at Columbia, but of his loneliness in Toluca, and his inability to please his father or help his mother escape a life of poverty and struggle. Impulsively, he began to fling his books into the sea, feeling that he was throwing away not books but "a million bricks out of my heart." Exulting in the wind, the smell of the sea, and the sight of his books sinking under the waves, Hughes experienced the thrill of being "a man on my own, [who would] control my own life, and go my own way" (BS 98).

The entire voyage would take six months, but it took three weeks in pleasant weather to cross the Atlantic and reach Senegal. From there, the ship steamed southward down the African coast until reaching Sierra Leone, where an African crew of Kru tribesmen was taken on board. Hughes was surprised to learn that this crew was not only assigned the hard labor of loading and unloading cargo, but also several other duties, including much of his own work as a messman. The ship continued southward, calling at 32 different ports along the West Coast. At times it left the coast and journeyed up various rivers, most notably the Congo.

Hughes tried to befriend the Kru people and to compare the situation of Africans facing oppression from white foreigners to that of black Americans in the U.S. South. To his consternation, the Africans, seeing his relatively light skin color, refused to recognize him as other than a white man. Sensing his confusion, one man from Liberia explained that the few people of mixed blood found on the West Coast of Africa were generally either foreign missionaries who came to teach the people what they did not want or need to know, or administrators of white colonial law (*BS* 103).

The Africans' inability to see him as a black man, which later led to the Kru refusing to let him witness one of their religious ceremonies, underscored a dilemma Hughes faced. Throughout his African journey, Hughes would feel horror and indignation at the exploitation of Africa by Europeans and Americans and yet struggle with his own complicity. For example, he was scandalized to learn that the Kru workers, who were doing part of his job along with the most backbreaking labor, were paid only two shillings a day, in contrast to his own $35 a month. As a messman he upheld the color line, feeding all the white officers of the ship before serving the local customs men and clerks, who were usually Africans. He resisted only once, when a white officer came late and tried to throw out the African clerks and officials who were already eating (*BS* 114–15). In poems and in various memoirs he wrote movingly of the plight of the young girls forced by poverty to sell themselves to the sailors, but apparently he sometimes joined the other crew members in visiting the brothels. In one particularly pathetic story that he relates in *The Big Sea*, he describes how two very young girls rowed themselves out to their ship, which had been anchored far offshore for about a week. The crew had not been allowed to go ashore and thus had not been issued any money, but the girls were unaware of this. One of the girls was taken by the boatswain to his cabin; the other was quickly surrounded by the rest of the crew on the deck. Hughes describes how they took turns raping her, refusing to allow her to leave, even though they had no money to pay. After awhile he left the deck, unable to bear her cries for "mon-nee," but the other sailors continued their sport for hours (108).

If he could not do anything to end the suffering he saw in Africa, he could at least write about it. In "The White Ones" Hughes indicts the "strong white ones" for torturing the people of Africa (*CP* 37). In "Dream Variations" (*CP* 40) he took a more symbolic approach:

> To fling my arms wide
> In some place of the sun,
> To whirl and to dance
> Till the white day is done.
> Then rest at cool evening
> Beneath a tall tree

While night comes on gently,
Dark like me
That is my dream! (1–9)

The speaker yearns to escape the "white day" and celebrates the night as "Dark like me" or "Black like me," reaffirming that identity with the African people that the Kru tribesman dismissed. In "Brothers," Hughes asserts the relationship between all dark-skinned people whether they be West Indians, African Americans, or Africans (CP 424).

In October, having discharged the Kru crewmen at Sierra Leone, the ship began the return crossing. Langston, along with many of his fellow crewmen, had acquired a pet monkey on the voyage, and chaos ensued when a storm demolished the cage on deck that had been made for the monkeys, sending them scurrying up the masts and all over the ship. Despite continued bad weather that pushed the ship off course, the *West Hesseltine* reached Brooklyn in two weeks. Food supplies had run low because of unchecked raiding by the crew, and Hughes and the others were eager to get their pay and get off the ship, not caring that the whole crew was summarily fired for its undisciplined behavior on the voyage.

Back in Harlem, Hughes could not find a boarding house that would accept his monkey, whom he had named Jocko, and had to spend some of his hard-earned pay to board him at a pet shop. Although he had planned to spend only a few days in Harlem, an advertisement for a performance of Eleonora Duse, the legendary Italian actress, changed his mind, even though it meant delaying his departure to see his family in McKeesport for two weeks. Careful with his money, Hughes nevertheless found it impossible not to dip into the $50 he had set aside for Carrie. He bought a new suit and attended Duse's performance as part of the standing-room crowd, but was disappointed in the show. She was older than he expected; he did not understand Italian, and her voice barely reached him. He was too far away to be moved by her gestures and expressions.

When he went to retrieve Jocko he was astonished and angry to be charged $30 rather than the few dollars he had expected for the monkey's board. He finally made it to McKeesport with no money to spare, having had to sell the extra pair of pants that came with his new suit to raise the last few dollars of his fare. Hughes made Jocko a present to his adopted brother, Kit, who quickly grew attached after initially being frightened. Carrie was less than pleased, however, and the monkey caused various kinds of trouble with in-laws, neighbors, and for Carrie herself. Soon after Hughes returned to New York, she sold the monkey to a pet shop.

Chapter 5

EUROPEAN ADVENTURE

Back in Harlem, Langston felt uncertain about his future. During his stay in McKeesport he had given a reading of his poetry at a YMCA and discovered that his trip to Africa made him more interesting to his audience. While he was in Africa, his reputation in literary Harlem had increased. The *Crisis* had devoted a whole page of the August issue to his poems and Langston found himself warmly welcomed by a circle of black writers working in Harlem. Jessie Fauset had started a novel; Toomer was basking in the fame attending his recent publication of *Cane*; the Harlem Branch Library was hosting a series of lectures and readings. The atmosphere was exciting, but Hughes needed to support himself. Should he look for another berth or take Cullen's suggestion and try for a scholarship to Howard University? Cullen hinted that Locke might be eager to help with such a plan. In fact Locke, at Cullen's urging, sent Hughes a letter inviting him to come to Washington and help him with his research.

Hughes was still uneasy about accepting any favors from Locke and instead signed onto the *McKeesport* as a messman. The ship headed for Rotterdam in a December snowstorm, arriving just before Christmas and returning a month later. The trip had been cold and miserable but Langston enjoyed Rotterdam. Trying out his French on some of the people he met during his trip had renewed his desire to see Paris. Back in New York, Hughes celebrated his 22nd birthday with Cullen and, acting on impulse after reading over Locke's letters, he sent him a telegram asking if he could come to him. When Locke did not immediately reply by telegram, as perhaps Hughes had expected, Hughes had second thoughts. He sent an embarrassed and apologetic second message letting

Locke know that he would try to meet him some other time but would leave on the ship again, on February 5th. The weather on this trip to Holland was even worse than on the previous journey, and Hughes wondered if he had made the right choice. According to Rampersad, after a quarrel with the steward, who refused to allow Langston to eat any of the leftover chicken that was reserved for officers, Langston resolved to desert the ship. Taking a $20 advance on his pay, Hughes went ashore for the ship's holiday and never came back; instead he boarded a train for Paris (*LLH* I: 83).

Arriving in Paris with only seven dollars remaining, Hughes's first task was to find a job, but the results of his search were discouraging. While there was a demand for black musicians, he was told that there were "plenty of French people" available to wait tables or wash dishes or be janitors (*BS* 146). Meanwhile the expense of food and lodging was steadily draining his funds. His luck improved when he met a woman he called Sonya, a Russian émigré-dancer also looking for work. She helped him find a cheap apartment and invited herself to move in after he paid for two weeks. Within days she found a job and they both ate on her salary until Hughes was hired as a doorman at a small nightclub, which paid only five francs a night, but also provided dinner.

Sonya took a job dancing at Le Havre, and Hughes was once more alone. Not liking the low pay and the expectation that he would also act as a bouncer, Hughes was relieved to find a better job as a dishwasher, or nominally the second cook, at the Grand Duc nightclub where his salary was tripled.

In the spring, Hughes befriended four young, black British women, among them, Anne Marie Cousey, whom he calls "Mary" in *The Big Sea*. Cousey was studying weaving and French in Paris and was resisting family pressure to marry an English suitor who did not quite measure up to her ideal. She hinted that Langston was closer to her ideal, but he was careful to avoid serious entanglement even as he wrote to his friends about being in love. Anne was pushing him to return home and continue his education, while he was in no hurry to leave France. They quarreled over whether his Paris interlude was contributing to his growth as a poet. In the meantime his reputation back in America continued to grow as Cullen helped to place some of the poems he had written while in Africa. His poetry appeared not only in the *Crisis*, but also in the *Messenger* and the new magazine *Opportunity: A Journal of Negro Life*. Hughes began to experiment with jazz rhythms in the poetry he wrote while in France, even though both Cullen and Jessie Fauset disapproved of these free verse experiments.

Cousey left to go home to England without any definite proposal from Hughes. Hughes wrote some sentimental lyrics after she left in which he mourned his lost love, and he later wrote in his autobiography as if they had been separated by her father. The evidence suggests, however, that he actually may have been somewhat relieved to end the relationship. He did not accept an invitation to visit her in Hampstead. Meanwhile Hughes had continued to write to Locke, who showed up unexpectedly at his room one day in July. Hughes was flattered to be taken out to lunch by Locke, who talked of editing a special issue of the magazine *Survey Graphic* that was to focus on "the Negro question" and in which he wanted to publish some of Hughes's poetry. They spent a week together in Paris with Locke hinting at his desire for a more intimate relationship, and Hughes apparently resisting, yet not completely pushing Locke away because of his ability to help Hughes get into Howard University. Locke proposed that Hughes live with him back in Washington and attend Howard in the fall.

Hughes then left Paris to take a previously planned trip to the home of one of the Italian waiters at the club. Locke met Hughes again in Venice. Hughes soon tired of Locke's company and slipped away to see a little of the seedy side of Venice by himself. He began to rethink the plan of living with Locke and wondered how to extricate himself from an awkward situation. Providentially, Hughes's passport was stolen as their train approached Genoa. Locke crossed into France without him and continued on to the United States, leaving Langston to solve the problem of how to get home.

Hughes now found himself stranded in Genoa with little money. Faith Berry notes that the account in *The Big Sea* exaggerates his poverty there, for initially he wrote to Locke that everything was so inexpensive in Genoa that his money would easily last a month (*BS* 53). Unfortunately, his stay lasted six weeks. He could not find a berth on a ship bound for the United States because the American ships he applied to would not accept a black crewman. This bitter experience inspired the poem "I, Too" in which the speaker, the "darker brother," protests being forced to eat in the kitchen, but predicts a day when he will be welcomed at the table, his beauty recognized and the shame of racism exposed (*CP* 46). He also wrote "Burutu Moon," a prose piece recalling his time in Africa, and sent it to the *Crisis* begging for immediate payment. Before he heard anything from the magazine he found a ship with an all-black crew, the *West Cawthon*, which brought him home in exchange for work as a chipper, someone who helps maintain the boat by chipping away rust. He reached home in November 1924 and found the "Harlem Renaissance" gathering

steam. The term refers to the outpouring of literary and artistic achievements by African Americans based in Harlem from about 1925 to 1930,
and Hughes would be one of its central figures.[1]

Note

1. Although the Harlem Renaissance is primarily identified with the second half of the
1920s, many scholars include the entire decade and part of the next in that term. W. E. B.
DuBois wrote an editorial in the *Crisis* calling for "a renaissance of American Negro Literature" in 1920, and George Hutchinson points out that "significantly more single-
authored works of African American [creative writing] appeared in the 1930s than the
1920s" (384–85). Victor A. Kramer suggests that the Harlem Renaissance had far-
reaching effects that kept it "figuratively alive" through the 1970s (Kramer and Russ 5),
and several critics have found links between the Harlem Renaissance and the Black Arts
movement of the 1960s.

Chapter 6

"TRYING TO CATCH A JAZZ RHYTHM"

Though he arrived in New York nearly penniless, Hughes was welcomed warmly by the Cullen family at whose home he settled temporarily. He found much excitement in the black literary community. Fauset had just published her first novel, *There Is Confusion,* and Walter White had brought out *The Fire in the Flint* to much acclaim. In addition to the *Crisis*, Charles Johnson's *Opportunity* magazine, founded the previous year by the Urban League and in which one of Hughes's poems had recently appeared, was dedicated to publishing talented young, black writers. Furthermore, living up to the journal's name, Johnson had begun hosting large dinners and literary contests, which served to bring promising black writers to the attention of wealthy, prominent whites who might then be a source of patronage or an avenue for publication. At one such dinner, held while Langston was still in Paris, Johnson had presented Locke to the guests as the leader of the new literary movement in Harlem. Hughes found himself considered an important member of this movement. Thanks in part to Countee Cullen's efforts in placing his work while he was in Europe, Hughes's own reputation now rivaled Cullen's.

At a benefit party for the NAACP, which Hughes attended on the night he returned to New York, he learned from Augustus Dill that the *Crisis* had sent money for "Burutu Moon" and the check had just missed him in Genoa. Walter White, the novelist and an official of the NAACP, invited him to sit at his table. But the most important aspect of that party for Hughes was his introduction to Carl Van Vechten, a white music critic and author who would become one of his closest friends and an important link to the publishing world. A few days later at another party where he was again the center of admiring attention, he made the acquaintance of Arna Bontemps, a teacher at Harlem Academy and an aspiring writer who would also become a dear friend and frequent collaborator. Bontemps resembled Hughes physically and had even been mistaken for him previously when he went to call on Cullen (Bontemps 18). Cullen, Bontemps, and Hughes left the party together and spent the rest of the evening discussing poetry, especially Langston's (Bontemps 20).

Ironically, shortly after making these new friends Langston lost an old one, or rather, chose to end his friendship with Countee Cullen for reasons he kept private. Rampersad proposes that Cullen might have made a sexual overture to Hughes, revealing in the process that Locke had shared intimate details of his own pursuit of Langston. It would have been the violation of his privacy rather than the unwanted advance that caused him uncharacteristically to break off the relationship. In any case, Langston abruptly ended the friendship and makes no mention of his formerly close relationship with the other poet in his autobiography.[1]

No longer wanting to live with Locke, Langston had not yet given up on the idea of Howard University. He wanted to go back to college to increase his knowledge of history, psychology, and sociology, which would help him understand the world and human behavior. In this sense he thought a college education would help him become a better writer. However, this time he was determined that it be a Negro college, for he wished to understand and write about the experiences of black people. Although Langston, who could not even afford both a new overcoat and a train ticket to Washington, had little prospect of raising the tuition money, he was able to move to Washington, D.C., since his mother and stepbrother were already staying there at the home of some wealthy cousins, who had invited Langston to join them.

Introduced to a world of prosperous middle-class blacks, Hughes found them snobby and boring and felt they were laughing at him. He struggled for a while to find the kind of "dignified" job his relatives expected, such as becoming a page in the Library of Congress. Next, he unsuccessfully tried to sell ads for the *Washington Sentinel*, a black paper. Quitting that unprofitable job, he took a $12-a-week position at a laundry right after the *Crisis* published the poem "Song to a Negro Wash-Woman" (*CP* 41). His relatives liked neither the job nor the poem, and his mother was sensitive to their criticisms. Soon he, his mother, and Kit moved into a two-room apartment with no heat. They bought an oil stove that they moved back and forth from room to room in order to keep the whole apartment passably warm. With the added expense of housing, saving enough money for college was impossible.

Although he eventually found a higher paying and more prestigious job working for Carter G. Woodson, editor of the *Journal of Negro History*, Langston was not happy with the work. He was expected not only to provide general office help while attending to the furnace, the mail, the cleaning, and locking up in the evenings, but also to work as a clerk on Woodson's project, a compilation of *Thirty Thousand Free Negro Heads of Families in the United States in 1830*. Hughes's tedious assignment was to arrange in alphabetical order the cards on which the names of these 30,000 individuals were typed.

Hughes was also distressed by the level of segregation in Washington, which excluded him from seeing new movies or plays or even buying a cup of coffee downtown. Hughes was further outraged by the lack of objections from the "leading Washington Negroes" who claimed to have their own society and thus did not care to mingle with whites (*BS* 206). But to Hughes this society was pretentious and full of its own color and class lines. The lighter-skinned elite looked down scornfully on those with dark complexions or who lacked college degrees or held menial jobs. Indeed it was this kind of snobbery directed at Carrie that had led Langston and his mother to move out of her cousins' house.

Distancing himself from black "society," Hughes spent time in the slum areas on Seventh Street and was moved by the hymns he heard in the storefront churches and the blues and jazz he heard in the taverns and clubs. He tried to write poems that captured the moods of this music. Indeed his writing was the one thing that was going well. He published more poems than ever before in the year and two months he spent in the capital city, many of them with a socialist message, in such publications as the *Messenger* and the *Workers Monthly*. One of the poems was "Cross" in which a mulatto speaker describes his feelings toward his parents and toward being "neither white nor black" (*CP* 58–59).

In the spring of 1925 a special issue of the *Survey Graphic* titled "Harlem: Mecca of the New Negro" was edited by Alain Locke. Locke cited one of Hughes's poems, "Youth," to express the psychology of the new Negro. This poem is a hopeful call to march toward a future "Bright before us / Like a flame" (*CP* 39). The issue, later revised and republished as the book *The New Negro*, included 10 of Hughes's poems. This was a triumph for Langston, but it also brought about a new embarrassment. A group called the Literature Lovers of D.C. organized a formal dinner for some of the younger writers whose work was published in the special issue and invited Hughes, graciously conceding that he need not wear formal attire if he would only honor them with a reading of a few of his poems. The organizers, however, would not make an exception for his mother to attend without formal wear, and so Hughes boycotted the dinner.

Hughes began attending Saturday evening literary gatherings held at the home of Georgia Douglass Johnson. There he met talented black writers and actors, many of whom were pursuing careers in law, medicine, or civil service, despite their literary aspirations. *Opportunity* magazine was holding a literary contest that spring, and most of the participants in Johnson's salon entered. Hughes submitted several poems, including his long unpublished poem "The Weary Blues." At the end of April, Hughes fell ill and decided to skip the banquet in New York where the prize would be announced. Jessie Fauset, however, insisted that he go and lent him the money herself, so certain was she that he would win a prize. The banquet was held in a Fifth Avenue restaurant packed with black writers and representatives of white publishing houses. When the awards for poetry were announced, poems by Hughes and Cullen tied for third place. Cullen took second place and Hughes won first prize for "The Weary Blues." Langston was thrilled to hear his poem read aloud by James Weldon Johnson, the poet, novelist, and diplomat who was also general secretary for the NAACP. After the dinner he met a fellow prizewinner, Zora Neale Hurston, who impressed him as a bright, young woman whom he would like to know better (Bernard 19). He was also congratulated by Carl Van Vechten, who was immersing himself in black culture and regularly held integrated parties. At Van Vechten's urging, Hughes visited him the next day with a manuscript of his poems. He agreed to leave the manuscript with Van Vechten, who suggested some changes and offered to try to find him a publisher. Van Vechten soon secured a contract from Knopf and permission from Langston to write the introduction. In return, Langston provided material for some articles Van Vechten was writing for *Vanity Fair*, which also agreed to publish a selection of poems from the book in which Hughes "tried to catch the Jazz rhythm" (qtd. in *LLH* I:111). This was the first time that Hughes was paid for his poems.

Van Vechten pressed Langston for some details about his life that he could use to write the introduction. Langston provided a short autobiographical essay to which he gave a French title, "L'histoire de ma vie" (The Story of My Life). Van Vechten was so impressed that he showed the essay to Blanche Knopf and proposed that Hughes should write his autobiography. She was interested, and Langston reluctantly agreed to try to work on it, given Van Vechten's conviction that it would sell. However, he felt it would take time away from his poetry and was not especially eager to relive in detail the hardships of his early years, nor did he feel comfortable writing about the people who had influenced the course of his life and were still linked to him for good or ill (qtd. in Bernard 18). He also entered the *Crisis* awards competition and in August won a third place in poetry and a second place in the essay competition for an essay "The Fascination of Cities." The *Vanity Fair* issue featuring four of his jazz poems came out in September.

Langston was accepted to Howard, but despite his literary successes he could not get Howard to offer him a scholarship and he could not afford the tuition. He tried to work seriously on his autobiography but made little progress. He lived for a little while at the YMCA, then moved back home where his mother nagged him about his future. He had quit the job with Dr. Woodson, and Carrie was not impressed with the idea of his writing full time rather than taking a job where he could earn some money. In October, he gave in to the pressure and took a job as a busboy at the Wardman Park Hotel. The job paid $55 a month and gave him free afternoons to write. Clinging to his dream of attending college, he approached Carl Van Vechten, Walter White, and Jessie Fauset about helping him find a loan. Van Vechten was less than encouraging initially, suggesting that college would be a waste of time for Hughes, who should be working on his autobiography. Jessie Fauset was happy to recommend various educational funds to which he might apply, but Langston resisted her attempts to convince him not to choose a black school. Fauset assured him he would make much better contacts if he followed Countee Cullen's example and went to Harvard, where Cullen had just been admitted to graduate school. Defiantly, Langston applied to Lincoln University for the spring semester even though he did not yet have the funds to attend. On his application essay he wrote, "I *must* go to college in order to be of more use to my race and America" (qtd. in *LLH* I:116). He was accepted, but how would he raise the funds?

Hughes demonstrated an unexpected talent for self-promotion when he read in the newspaper that the poet Vachel Lindsay was staying at the Wardman Park Hotel and would give a public reading. Hughes looked for him in the dining room and left three of his poems beside his plate. He could not attend the reading himself because the auditorium did not admit blacks, but that night Lindsay opened his reading by stating that he had "discovered" a talented poet working as a busboy, and then read the three poems aloud. The story, first published in the local papers, was picked up by the Associated Press, and white reporters came to the hotel to interview Hughes. Hughes arranged further publicity by posing in his busboy's uniform for a photograph that was widely reprinted.

In late November, with the publication of *The Weary Blues* drawing near, Hughes traveled to New York to meet his publishers and attend a large party that Van Vechten threw in his honor. The next day he went to call on Amy Spingarn. Spingarn was the woman who had donated the money for the *Crisis* poetry contest, and Langston had previously written to thank her for her generosity, prompting her to invite him to visit her the next time he was in Manhattan. Hughes had just met her brother-in-law, Arthur Spingarn, at Van Vechten's party. When Hughes confided his financial difficulties, Amy Spingarn offered him $300 to fund his first year at Lincoln. Hughes would enroll when the new semester began in February.

Hughes quit his busboy job and sold a few poems to the *New Republic* and the *Herald Tribune*. One advantage of breaking into "white" publications was that they paid for contributions. But Hughes was still primarily interested in reaching a black audience. When his book *The Weary Blues* came out in January 1926, Hughes quarreled with Blanche Knopf over her decision to advertise the book only in white publications. Langston himself marketed the book to both black and white audiences by giving several successful readings and signing copies for hundreds of eager admirers. Ambivalent about all the attention, Hughes was somewhat relieved to escape to Lincoln University. He wrote jokingly to Van Vechten that he hoped to find no poetry lovers in the seclusion of Lincoln (Bernard 36).

Note

1. Rampersad comments that Hughes "snapped this [friendship] in two" and indeed Hughes and Cullen were never as close again as they were in their youth (*LLH* I: 98). Nevertheless, the rift was smoothed over to some degree after each poet praised the other's first book of poetry, and by the time Hughes was at Lincoln University, he was corresponding with Cullen again. Hughes was in Cullen's wedding party and Rampersad notes that they were friendly with each other in Paris in the late 1930s (*LLH* I: 363).

Chapter 7

A RISING NEGRO ARTIST

If Lincoln University seemed to offer Hughes a welcome respite from the hectic pace of public readings and book signings to promote *The Weary Blues*, it also offered something more precious—one of his first experiences (other than his segregated elementary-school years) of being at school only with other black people. Langston sought this, much as he had sought to live in Harlem a few years earlier. Then, he had felt that the desire to get a college education had drawn him "to the hill above Harlem," away from his own people. Now he could pursue this dream and still immerse himself in black culture.

Lincoln University, located in Pennsylvania, with an enrollment of about 300 students, was fairly prestigious among black colleges and had graduated many lawyers, doctors, and clergymen. The tenured faculty were all white, a circumstance that Hughes would come to protest. The school admitted only male students, but they were allowed more freedom than at many black colleges, which tended to have strict rules governing student behavior. While he eagerly took up college life, taking classes in French, Spanish, algebra, and English and American literature and pledging the fraternity Omega Psi Phi, Hughes still kept one foot in Harlem. He often traveled on weekends to Manhattan and other cities to give readings of his work and sometimes arranged performances at black churches and schools in which he appeared with his school's vocal quartet. He performed in his old hometown of Cleveland where several former classmates and teachers were in the audience. He was also invited to give a reading at Oberlin College and performed with both the vocal quartet and the glee club at Lincoln itself. At some of these readings he sold copies of *The Weary Blues*, which had received generally favorable reviews and had gone into a second printing. By the summer when he received his first royalty check (for $124.17 after advances and fees for personal copies were deducted), the book had sold 1,628 copies (*LLH* I: 131).

Just as Hughes was taking his exams, a letter arrived from Freda Kirchwey, editor of the *Nation*. She enclosed proofs of George Schulyer's "Negro-Art Hokum," an essay scheduled to appear in the magazine, and asked Hughes for a counterstatement. Schulyer, editor of the *Pittsburgh Courier*, a prominent black newspaper, rejected the whole idea of "American Negro art." The best work in literature, sculpture, and painting produced by "AfraAmericans" was, in Schuyler's view, simply American and showed the same European influences as that produced by white Americans. Art forms associated with blacks such as spirituals, jazz, and the Charleston, were really only common to Southern Negroes and should be considered a kind of folk art "no more expressive or characteristic of the Negro race than the music and dancing of the Appalachian highlanders...[is] expressive or characteristic of the Caucasian race." He argued that it was ridiculous to assume that an artist's skin color rather than his environment and nationality influenced his work, and he maintained that the assertion that there is a peculiar Negro art is just a variation of the premise that "the blackamoor is inferior and fundamentally different."

Schulyer's views were provocative, and Hughes agreed to contribute a reply. His response was "The Negro Artist and the Racial Mountain," a significant statement of his philosophy that would become something of a manifesto for the Harlem Renaissance. Hughes opens the essay by lamenting the remark of Countee Cullen (though he identifies him only as a promising young Negro poet) to the effect that he wanted to be known not as a Negro poet, but simply as a poet. Hughes saw in this statement a desire to be white and a fear of his own racial identity that was not unique to Cullen. Hughes identified "the desire to pour racial individuality into the mold of American standardization, and to be as little Negro and as much American as possible" as the main obstacle restraining the development of blacks as artists. This is the "racial mountain" a black artist must scale in order to reach his potential.

Hughes further argued that the black middle class is the source of this desire to be white and be accepted by whites. In middle-class homes, the children are taught to hold themselves superior to those of their race with less education, money, and social status. White people are held up as models to imitate in order to be successful, and children are scolded for "acting like niggers" if they misbehave. A child raised in such a home is never taught to see "the beauty of his own people" and so can have little interest in making it the subject of art. The child may even be ashamed of anything that does not conform to white models.

However, Hughes celebrates the "low-down folks" who make up the majority of American blacks. These people do not waste time imitating whites or feeling ashamed of themselves. They throw themselves passionately into life. They hold onto their own distinctive identity, their own music, their own humor. A true black artist is more likely to come from these classes and/or to draw his material from their lives than from the middle-class blacks who are concerned with being respectable and acting like whites.

Times have been difficult for the black artist, however, because he or she finds such small encouragement from those blacks supposed to have more culture. For example, many respectable black churches refused to include spirituals in their worship. Why, Hughes asks, are European folk songs viewed as interesting cultural expressions while Negro folk songs are considered embarrassingly vulgar? He points out the irony that while "Negro art" had suddenly become popular, it took the interest of whites to make the so-called cultured Negroes take notice. He gives as an example the story of his own humiliating experience with the Literature Lovers of D.C. (though without identifying himself as the writer in question). It took the acceptance of his work by a white press to make the "best" Negroes in the city pay attention to him, and then they "honored" him with a dinner from which his own mother was excluded so that they could uphold their artificial standards of dress.

Hughes points out that even with this new surge of interest, truly daring work is met with suspicion: whites want the Negro artist to conform to, not challenge, their stereotypes, while middle-class blacks want him to be respectable and show blacks in a good light to whites. Listening to either group would compromise the black artist who must remain indifferent to the approval or disapproval of either. Hughes defends his own choice of racial themes and his use of jazz in his poetry. "Jazz to me is one of the inherent expressions of Negro life in America: the eternal tom-tom beating in the Negro soul—the tom-tom of revolt against weariness in a white world, a world of subway trains, and work, work, work; the tom-tom of joy and laughter, and pain swallowed in a smile." For Hughes the duty of the black artist is to conquer the racial mountain, to say through his work and thus help his audience to say as well, "Why should I want to be white? I am a Negro—and beautiful!" ("The Negro Artist").

Schuyler's essay appeared in the June 16, 1926, issue of the *Nation* and Hughes's followed a week later. Langston was paid for that contribution and also received a prize of $150 in July when his poem "A House in Taos" won the first prize in the Poetry Society of America contest for undergraduate poets. Meanwhile, pleased with Langston's progress in his first semester at Lincoln, Amy Spingarn agreed to finance him with another $400 for each year of his college career. His finances reasonably secure, Hughes was able to devote the summer of 1926 to writing projects.

He moved into a rented room in Wallace Thurman's house in Harlem and began to work on writing a revue for producer Caroline Dudley Reagan, who had previously taken a black revue to Paris. Van Vechten had recommended Hughes for the project, which was to star the popular black actor Paul Robeson. He also began to work with Zora Neale Hurston on a folk opera, but he finished neither project.

Hurston coined the term "Niggerati" to describe the group of young, black artists that included herself, Bruce Nugent, Wallace Thurman, Aaron Douglas, Gwendolyn Bennett, Dorothy West, Helene Johnson, John P. Davis, Countee Cullen, and Langston Hughes. Van Vechten was considered an honorary member, providing introductions, encouragement, and sometimes, financial assistance to the others, but he was about to become controversial. His involvement with the Harlem Renaissance had always been resisted by those who felt that he was exploiting the young artists for his own financial gain. Now his book *Nigger Heaven* was published to scathing reviews, especially in the black press, though it became a best seller.

DuBois's review in the *Crisis* was typical. The book was criticized for being too sensational. Many objected to the title. Some black newspapers refused to advertise it. But many of the younger writers saw the attack on Van Vechten as an attack on their own aspiration to write of black life without idealizing it, to write with freedom, and to celebrate the black masses. Thurman, Hughes, and several others decided to start their own magazine dedicated to publishing the kind of work they wanted to write. They chose the name *Fire!* and Hughes was among those contributing $50 toward the cost of the first issue.

Back at Lincoln in the fall of 1926, Hughes collected poems for his second book and again discussed his manuscript with Van Vechten, to whom he dedicated the collection. He was also able to help his friend with legal troubles by composing original blues lyrics to replace those that Van Vechten had included without attribution in his novel. Paid $100 for this work, Hughes sent some of the money to help Thurman meet further expenses for *Fire!*, which predictably came out to mixed reactions, including once again the charges of sensationalism and immorality. Continued financial troubles for the magazine meant that only this one issue ever appeared.

Knopf accepted Langston's second book but had qualms about the title, *Fine Clothes to the Jew*. Van Vechten supported the choice, which was a quotation from the poem "Hard Luck" and refers to having to pawn one's best clothes in order to raise money. Knopf agreed to publish the book under that title. Rampersad suggests that the title was probably chosen by Van Vechten in the first place, and that the controversial title contributed to the book's poor sales (*LLH* I: 138).

A further sign of the growing esteem in which Hughes was held as a poet was the request from Louis Untermeyer to include some of Hughes's poems in his revision of his anthology *Modern American and British Poetry*. Edwin Markham also included some of the poems in an anthology he was preparing. Hughes was invited to be a judge for the second *Crisis* awards competition.

So far, Hughes's reputation was built on his poetry and a few essays, but in the spring of 1927 he turned to writing short stories again. Perhaps part of the impetus was that he enrolled in a class on "The Short Story" at Lincoln, but he began writing before the semester started. He wrote a series of four stories (though he had planned six) all set on a ship sailing to Africa. He placed one with Thurman in his new magazine *Harlem*, and George Schuyler, the new editor of the *Messenger* and Hughes's opponent in the debate over "Negro Art," published the other three.

As the publication day for *Fine Clothes to the Jew* drew near, Hughes fretted about the possible reactions to his new book, which was focused on the lower classes. Would black critics respond as they had to Van Vechten? Indeed the book was harshly attacked. Hughes was a "sewer dweller," proclaimed one headline. Hughes was criticized for an obsessive focus on the seamy side of Negro life, of exposing blacks to the criticism of whites by depicting them as prostitutes and drunkards. Hughes responded to his critics in the *Pittsburgh Courier* and elsewhere by pointing out, as he had already in his essay for the *Nation*, that lower-class blacks were the majority of American black people, and he strongly disagreed that writers should only portray their "higher selves" in any case. If his poems were "indelicate," then so was life. As for the charge of ugliness, Hughes explained in the *Cleveland Plain Dealer* that if some of his poems contained ugliness, it was in order to protest that ugliness rather than to dwell on it (qtd. in *LLH* I: 144–45).

Despite the controversy and low sales of his book, it is considered one of Hughes's best. True to the philosophy he expressed in "The Negro Artist and the Racial Mountain," Hughes sought to capture the essence of African American life as lived by its common people. Hughes eschews traditional lyric forms and conventional poetic language. Nearly all the poems are in the form of the blues lyrics, most often voiced by a woman. Most focus on sorrow and suffering but a few voice joy and a passionate sexuality.

Hughes's last two years at Lincoln were easier than the first two because in the late spring of 1927 he was introduced to a wealthy woman who would become his patron. Her generous funding released him from the constant need to supplement his stipend from Amy Spingarn. With a new source of income, Hughes was able to refuse offers to read to ladies' clubs and provincial literary societies. In these years, Hughes continued to win honors and have his poems translated, selected for anthologies, and set to music, but he wasn't writing important new poems. As we will see in the next chapter, his major creative energies went into writing his novel, *Not Without Laughter*, which was in draft form when he finished Lincoln.

In his senior year he also found time to write a controversial study of Lincoln for his sociology class in which he criticized the absence of black faculty and trustees and the effect that it had on the self-image of students there, who were largely opposed to the hiring of black faculty. He graduated in June 1929 but did not go far. He had secured the permission of the president to remain on campus free of charge for the summer in order to have a quiet place to work on revising his novel for publication.

Chapter 8

PARK AVENUE GODMOTHER

Although Hughes had not been particularly interested in writing a novel, he began one at the behest of his patron, Charlotte Mason, to whom Locke had introduced him in 1927. Mason was an elderly, wealthy white woman who wished to become a patron of black writers and artists. After attending a lecture by Locke on African art, Mason had introduced herself to him and confided her dream of creating a black art museum and of resurrecting the original African culture among African Americans. As she herself explained in a letter to Locke written in 1932, she wanted, through her museum and sponsorship of black artists, to erect a "bridge" by which black Americans could travel culturally back to Africa and reclaim the heritage from which they had been severed by years of oppression by American whites (qtd. in *LLH* I: 147–48). Locke also spoke to her of the literary movement that he was guiding and nurturing, and she wished to be introduced to some of these young writers. Hughes was one of the first that Locke invited to meet Mrs. Mason, and she immediately took an interest in him and presented him with $50. After visiting Mason a second time and listening to her theories, Hughes was asked to call her "Godmother."

Hughes cultivated the relationship by writing to her that summer as he headed south. He began by reading his poems at the Fisk University commencement exercises, then visited Memphis, and planned to go to Texas where he had secured a reading engagement at a YWCA conference. A flood cancelled the conference, and so he traveled by train to Mississippi and Louisiana instead. In July, he encountered Zora Neale Hurston in Alabama. She was touring the South in her own car, collecting material for her research. Together they spent several more weeks driving through the rural South, visiting with people, and collecting their folk songs and stories. Hughes and Hurston returned to the idea of collaborating on a folk opera which they had begun discussing the summer before.

Upon returning to New York, Langston was eager to see Godmother. He shared his experiences and, telling her about Hurston, suggested that they meet. Godmother urged him to write a novel about the summer's travels. Hughes was reluctant but pretended enthusiasm so as not to disappoint Godmother. Back at Lincoln, however, he found it difficult to concentrate on writing at all. When he confided this to Godmother, she proposed to support him with a monthly stipend.

The arrangement was that Godmother would pay Hughes $150 per month beginning in November 1927, and Hughes would discuss his creative work with her and report his expenses. He was not to reveal her identity to anyone without her permission. She also started a similar arrangement with Hurston soon after. Godmother encouraged Hughes to write in a racially conscious but primitive style. He should cultivate a connection with Africa as a spiritual source. Hughes, however, was more interested in socialism and the realities of black American life in the twentieth century.

This artistic disagreement was only one source of tension between them. Hughes also resented having to track and report his spending. Perhaps this reminded him of his past battles with his father. True, Godmother was supporting him in his literary endeavors as his father had never done, but like his father she was trying to impose her vision of his future on him rather than affirming his own. As he explained in *The Big Sea*, "I was not Africa. I was Chicago and Kansas City and Broadway and Harlem" which was not "what she wanted me to be" (325).

Despite these potential problems, the relationship thrived at first. Hughes made frequent visits to Mrs. Mason's home on Park Avenue and escorted her to lectures, plays, and concerts. He dined luxuriously at her home, and she even paid to send Kit Clark to school in New England when Langston confided that his mother was having trouble managing the teenaged boy.

When the summer of 1928 arrived, Hughes put aside the distractions of college and finally settled down to work seriously on his novel. He may have become more enthusiastic because several acclaimed novels by Harlem writers were published in that year including McKay's *Home to Harlem*, Rudolph Fisher's *Walls of Jericho*, Jessie Fauset's *Plum Bun*, and Nella Larsen's *Quicksand*. Hughes planned to write a somewhat disguised autobiography but to make the central character a more typical southern black boy. He sent Godmother each chapter as he drafted it; she sent back words of encouragement. After finishing the first draft in late August, Hughes worked on a "singing play," *The Emperor of Haiti,* but he was unable to finish it before he returned to school for his final year.

When Godmother returned from a trip to Europe in the fall of 1928, she began pressing Hughes to revise the novel and reminded him that she had not received his financial records for October. He began to feel hounded. But it was not until February 1929 that their first real falling-out took place. Godmother invited him for lunch only to treat him to a dramatic outburst. She accused him of ingratitude and, in particular, of not thanking her enough for the leather bag she had given him for Christmas, as well as taking her money and producing nothing with it. Devastated, Hughes wrote her a letter of apology, saying he was sorry he had disappointed her and professing his continued love, but suggesting that perhaps they had better sever their relationship if he hurt her so much (qtd. in *LLH* I: 168–69). She was satisfied and accepted his apology, and so their arrangement continued.

Almost immediately after Hughes graduated from Lincoln in 1929, he returned to the campus to work quietly on his novel with Godmother's support. In addition to funding, she provided a lengthy criticism of the novel, which she found lacking in the qualities of "literary expression" and marred by lapses into self-conscious propaganda (qtd. in *LLH* I: 172). After working hard all summer, Hughes finished his second draft by mid-August and Godmother rewarded him with an extra $250 for travel to Maryland and Montreal.

Hughes met with Godmother in Manhattan in September. They both agreed that the novel still needed more revision. Hughes recalled that he had viewed the novel as finished, but when he reread it upon his return to New York, he saw that it still needed work. His characters were "locked up in long pages of uncomfortable words, awkward sentences, and drawn-out passages" (*BS* 305). Godmother believed that if Hughes lived in Harlem he would be too distracted to complete the revisions. So she found him a room in the home of a black couple in Westfield, New Jersey. Beginning in October, Louise Thompson was hired to work as his stenographer/typist for $150 per month, with Godmother paying the bill yet expecting Louise to send her thank-you notes for her patronage, as if she were another "godchild" (*LLH* I: 174).

Thompson was formerly a teacher at Hampton Institute, where she had met Hughes when he gave a reading there in March 1928. She came to New York that summer and was hired as typist by Wallace Thurman. In a matter of weeks, Thurman and Thompson were married, to the amazement of Thurman's friends who recognized his homosexual inclinations. To the surprise of no one, the marriage soon collapsed, but Thompson returned from Reno to New York without her divorce so that she could be near her mother, who was dying of cancer. Thompson continued to live with her mother in an apartment in New York, where Hughes brought the successive drafts to be typed.

Hughes renewed his friendship with Arna Bontemps, who was also working on a novel. Meanwhile he was still frequently called on to be Mason's escort. Hughes was a bit troubled by the pampered life he was leading while so many suffered in the aftermath of the stock market crash, but determined to retain Mason's support.

He pressed on with the novel, which Knopf agreed to publish. Now called *Not Without Laughter*, the book is the story of Sandy, a young black boy growing up in Kansas who is being raised primarily by his grandmother, Hagar. Sandy is a witness to the struggles between his grandmother and her youngest daughter, rebellious Harriet, who eventually runs away from home to become an entertainer. Sandy's father, like Langston's, is mostly absent, for he is unwilling to do the kind of work allotted to Negroes in the United States and is always moving on, looking for something better. Unlike James Hughes, however, Jimboy is not ashamed to be black and finds solace in playing the blues. Hagar's older daughter, Tempy, represents the kind of middle-class Negro woman that Hughes had criticized in "The Negro Artist and the Racial Mountain." Sandy lives with her for five years after Hagar's death before moving North to be with his mother at last, only to find that she expects him to quit school and help support her by working as an elevator operator. The characters in the story often discuss white folks and why they treat black folks so badly, and the novel contains vivid scenes of humiliations whites, sometimes unthinkingly, sometimes deliberately, inflict on blacks. Despite illuminating the hardships caused by poverty, racism, and limited opportunities, the novel celebrates black life and the spirit of those who realize that "no matter how hard life might be, it was not without laughter" (267).

Knopf's agreement to publish the book was a triumph; yet when Godmother invited Locke to read and criticize the draft Knopf had accepted, he urged further changes, and Godmother, too, was not quite satisfied. Wearily Hughes made more revisions. In February 1930, he turned over the final version of his novel to his publisher, glad finally to be rid of the book that Godmother had hounded him to write.

He decided to recuperate with a trip to Cuba where he hoped to find a musician who could collaborate with him on the unfinished *Emperor of Haiti*. Godmother was enthusiastic and gave him $500 for the trip. Unfortunately, Hughes had trouble getting any of the cruise lines to sell him tickets, as they were unwilling to take on black passengers. With the intervention of Walter White of the NAACP, he eventually secured a stateroom on the Cunard line. Hughes enjoyed himself in Cuba, where he was treated with great respect by Cuban writers who were eager to meet and talk to him. He was treated especially cordially by José Antonio Fernández de Castro, editor of the leading paper in Havana, *El Diario de la Marina*. Fernández de Castro had previously translated one of Hughes's poems into Spanish; he saw to it that Hughes met all the leading writers and intellectuals of Cuba, introducing him as America's greatest Negro poet. Hughes would have a powerful influence on the Cuban writer Nicolás Guillén, who soon began writing poems about Cuban blacks based on rhythms of Afro-Cuban music that were compared to Hughes's blues poems. However, Hughes was neither able to locate a composer, nor carry away any fresh inspiration for his own poetry.

Hughes returned from Cuba to find he had a new neighbor. Zora Neale Hurston was now also working in Westfield. Furthermore, Godmother now expected Thompson to do the typing for both of them. Hurston had spent the previous two years in the South but had written frequently to Hughes during that time, flattering him and referring to their plans to collaborate on a folk opera. Now they had the ideal opportunity to work together, but instead of an opera they began working on a play, a comedy set in an all-black town in the South. The origin of the plot was in a short story by Hurston called "The Bone of Contention." In Hurston's story, two hunters dispute which one has shot a large turkey, and one hits the other with a mule bone. Since one man is a Baptist and the other a Methodist, their respective churches get involved in the resulting trial. The assailant is convicted of assault with a deadly weapon on the grounds that if Samson killed a thousand Philistines with the jaw of an ass, then a mule bone must be an even more lethal instrument. The felon is banished from the town.

Hughes and Hurston expanded the story into a play, with Hughes proposing to change the cause of the dispute from a turkey to a woman. Hughes apparently was primarily responsible for the dramatic structure of the play (it was he who outlined each act) and for the content of the dialogue in regard to advancing the plot, while Hurston, with her knowledge of black, Southern folklore and humor, made sure the dialogue sounded authentic and added jokes, tall tales, and a proposing contest. The play was called *Mule Bone* and the two worked closely on it for several weeks.

Some secrecy was necessary at first because neither was sure whether Godmother would approve this project. First, there was not enough money to pay Thompson to do the typing on *Mule Bone*. Hurston was quite resistant to Hughes's suggestion that in lieu of payment the writers give Thompson a share of the royalties when the play was produced or agree to make her business manager of any eventual *Broadway* production, but Hurston did not make the full extent of her feelings known at the time. The other problem was that Mason became suspicious about their lack of progress on other projects and wondered whether they were taking their work seriously.

According to Rampersad, when Godmother first became angry it was apparently with Hurston, not Hughes, and Hughes tried to smooth things over by telephoning her on Hurston's behalf. She refused to take the call, which then led him to write a contrite letter in which he apologized for having disturbed her and begged her to blame himself, not Zora, for her displeasure. The letter, like the one he wrote in response to her angry outburst over the Christmas gift, expressed his bafflement over how he had managed to offend her when he only loved and wanted to please her and blamed his own stupidity for the problems between them (qtd. in *LLH* I: 183–84). Godmother eventually calmed down and the two writers explained their current project to her, obtaining her consent to have Thompson do the typing for the project.

In May, with the first and third acts completed and part of the second act finished, Hurston announced that she was moving back to Manhattan and would soon go south to do further anthropological research. She would also work on the second act, and they would resume their collaboration when she returned. With the *Mule Bone* project over for the time being, Hughes decided to take a brief trip to Washington at the end of May, over Godmother's objections. She believed he should stay home in Westfield and write, and they apparently had an angry scene before he caught his train, which left Hughes feeling nearly as ill as he had when he had tried to stand up to his father in Mexico.

Hughes struggled over how to repair his relationship with Godmother. According to his autobiography he sent her a letter asking "to be released from further obligations to her, and that she give [him] no more money, but simply let [him] retain her friendship" (*BS* 325). Extant drafts of letters Hughes wrote to Godmother at this time show Hughes struggling to express his feelings. In one draft dated June 6, he protests Godmother's apparent belief that her financial support gave her the right to dictate what and when he wrote. In another undated draft he praises her generosity and goodness and begs to be allowed to continue to see her (qtd. in LLH I: 184, 186).

For her part, she replied somewhat frostily that it was Hughes who had wanted to try the plan they had been following since November 1927, by which he received a monthly allowance and was accountable for his expenditures. Her other protégées were successful with this plan, but if Hughes had problems with it, then she was quite willing to dispense with keeping accounts. To prove that it was not she who was obsessed with money, she sent him a check for $250 with no strings attached (qtd. in *LLH* I:186–87). But when he tried to see her in person, she kept him at a distance, making him feel her continued displeasure. When Hughes received an invitation to be a dramatist-in-residence that fall with the Hedgerow Players, an experimental, predominantly black theater group run by Jasper Deeter in Rose Valley, Pennsylvania, he wrote eagerly to Godmother. But she sent a telegram refusing his request to meet with her and talk over the opportunity.

In July, Hughes sent her the first copy of *Not Without Laughter*, accompanied by a letter thanking her for her love and friendship. Mason acknowledged the gift without inviting him to see her. The novel got the most appreciative reviews of any book that Hughes had written thus far. Meanwhile, Hughes began to work with his other patron, Amy Spingarn, to publish a small book of poems on a handpress. Hughes selected a dozen poems including "Dear Lovely Death," which gave the collection its title.

Though he had determined to accept the Hedgerow position, Hughes was disappointed that Deeter had not been able to secure the funds for his planned season of Negro theater. Hughes stayed on anyway, watching rehearsals of *Devil's Disciple* and performances of *Othello* and *The Emperor Jones* and volunteering in the office for a few hours each day in exchange for room and board. Hughes showed Deeter the first act of the *Mule Bone* script and received some advice and encouragement. As he wrote to Arthur Spingarn, he was gratified when Deeter read the act aloud to his company (*MB* 231, 235).

Hughes also began drafting a play called "Cross: A Play of the Deep South" which was a development of the "tragic mulatto" theme of his poem "Cross." The play, which was subsequently retitled *Mulatto*, is a melodramatic story of a white Southerner who tolerates and provides for his children by his Negro housekeeper/mistress as long as they know their place. He clashes with one son, Bert, who insists on being recognized as his father's son and annoys the town by demanding to be treated with respect. The hostility between father and son erupts into violence and Bert kills his father and is himself lynched by a white mob.

Godmother mailed Hughes a check in September but with only a brief letter. While he had asked for her love without the money to come between them, he was getting some money but no love. The pain he felt at her rejection was acute. Hoping for reconciliation, he sent her the reviews

of his novel. He told her about the many illnesses he was suffering including tonsillitis, toothache, and stomach troubles, problems he would recognize in *The Big Sea* as psychosomatic ones brought on by his distress
over Godmother's coolness. The physical problems continued after his
stint at Hedgerow ended and he returned to New York.

Hughes was not the only one having problems with Godmother. Toward the end of September, Mason abruptly summoned Louise Thompson
to her apartment and fired her. Thompson was bewildered and hoped that
Hurston could explain things, but her phone had been disconnected.

Upon returning to New York, Hughes began trying to contact Hurston
and resume work on the play, but she claimed to be too busy. They had
corresponded during the fall and summer, but Hughes had not been
shown her revisions, and the time at Hedgerow had made him eager to
finish the script. Hurston seemed to be too preoccupied. As Hughes later
explained to Arthur Spingarn, sometimes she made appointments with
him and failed to show up; at others, she was able to talk with him only
briefly before rushing out. She did let him scan the second act that she
had written while down South, and Hughes noted that she had put references to the turkey back into the play, but she did not let him make a copy
and so their collaboration did not progress (MB 232).

In his autobiography, Hughes recalls a painful final meeting with Mrs.
Mason around this time (BS 325–28), but since no records exist to con-
firm this meeting, and the illnesses he claims followed from that meeting
had actually plagued him all summer and fall, it may be more probable
that, as Rampersad suggests, he was actually recalling the meeting that
preceded his journey to Washington the previous spring. In that case,
Hughes presents as a clean break the disintegration of a relationship that
actually took place over several months, during which Hughes made pa-
thetic attempts to regain Mrs. Mason's love and she held him at a distance
with occasional checks and impersonal replies (LLH I: 193). But
Langston was at last beginning to accept the end. It was perhaps a sign of
his despair that when the holiday season passed with no sign of Godmother's thawing toward him, he left for Cleveland without taking leave
of her.

Chapter 9

THE *MULE BONE* OF CONTENTION

Hughes settled into his mother's house in early January 1931. He was still feeling ill and planned a trip to Florida to recuperate. Despite her rift with Hughes, Mason had continued to send checks from time-to-time and she planned to finance his travel with a check expected momentarily. Instead, he received on January 10 a letter chiding him for leaving town without telling her and informing him that no more money would be sent.

Hughes tried to make the best of his stay in Cleveland, scheduling a lecture and reading at his alma mater and another lecture in Shaker Heights. He also called on old friends Rowena and Russell Jelliffe. Their Playground House, where Hughes had worked during high school as an art teacher, had evolved into Karamu House, named after the Swahili word for "the place of entertainment or feasting at the center of the community" (*LLH* I: 317). The Jelliffes had also formed an amateur, black drama troupe, the Gilpin Players, which performed at Karamu House.

Rowena surprised Hughes by telling him that her troupe was expecting to get the rights to a new Negro comedy written by Zora Neale Hurston called *Mule Bone*. She had not yet read the script, which was currently under consideration by the Theatre Guild also, but had been advised by Barrett Clark, who was handling the script for the Samuel French theatrical agency, that the Guild would probably reject it. Thus the Gilpin Players expected to receive the script within a week, giving them a month to rehearse before their season began on February 15. Shocked and indignant, Hughes explained that this was the play that he and Hurston had been working on. He could not understand why she would send it out unfinished and without consulting him. He immediately wrote to Hurston for an explanation and sent for his own copies of the play to be mailed to him from Westfield.

The script from Clark arrived on Friday, January 16, in a very confused state, according to the account Hughes gave Van Vechten a few days later. Act I had two different endings, and there were two different third acts. One version in each case was the one that had been completed in Westfield by the two of them the previous spring and the other was Hurston's revision (MB 218). In a letter to his lawyer, Arthur Spingarn, written on January 21, Hughes elaborates: in the first act Hurston had reinserted the turkey and moved the fight off-stage, changes that weakened the dramatic structure of the play. She had also included a new, slightly different ending with the comment that it might be better than the other (the one on which she and Hughes had collaborated). The second act was the one Hurston had briefly shown Hughes and that she had written in the South. Hughes insisted it was still based on notes he had made when they were working together. Finally, she sent two third acts; one was a carbon copy of the one they had done together and the other showed minor changes but had clearly been based on the older version (MB 233). Rowena Jelliffe, comparing the script with Langston's own, concluded that Hurston had evidently made some alterations to support a claim of having redone the play. But she dismissed these changes as "feeble" and felt certain that Hughes was still entitled to be recognized as a co-author (MB 258).

Having received no response to his first inquiry, Hughes had just sent Hurston another letter on the morning of January 16, prior to his receipt and review of the script, asking why she was being so evasive about the play and pleading with her to explain (MB 210). But now he was provoked into more aggressive action. He wrote to Carl Van Vechten asking for his advice, and despite his shortage of funds, some time that weekend, probably on Sunday evening, January 18, he made a long-distance phone call to Hurston.[1] The call apparently did not go well. Hughes was torn between his outrage over Hurston's attempt to claim their collaborative work as her own and his genuine desire to see the play produced by the Gilpin Players, for which he needed her consent. When Hurston, honestly shocked to learn that an amateur group in Cleveland was planning to put on her play, denied any knowledge of how the play had wound up being circulated by Samuel French, Hughes assumed she was lying. She, on the other hand, apparently suspected him of offering the older version of the play to the Gilpin Players without her consent, as a way of taking credit for what she saw as *her* play. While he distinguished between *our* version and *your* version, she insisted that both versions were hers. When he pressed her to admit to trying to sell their play without his knowledge or consent, Hurston said she would explain all that in a letter. Meanwhile, she didn't see why she should be eager to have the play produced in Cleveland by an amateur group.

Hughes felt a little better on Monday morning, January 19, after he and Rowena Jelliffe called Barrett Clark and discovered that Hurston was telling the truth. She had never met Clark and did not know that he had submitted the play either to the Theater Guild or the Gilpin Players. The play had been given to Clark by Carl Van Vechten. As Van Vechten explained in a letter to Hughes also written on January 19, Hurston had given him the play the previous November with a note claiming that she and Hughes had originally worked together on the idea, but then she had started over in Alabama and that she was the solitary author of the script she gave him (even though it actually contained all the work that they had done together as well as the revisions she had made). Van Vechten stated that he believed Hurston had behaved inappropriately and urged Hughes to consider legal action if Hurston would not acknowledge his rights (MB 215–17).

After talking to Clark, Hughes wrote and immediately mailed two letters. The first was to Hurston, and in it he took a conciliatory tone, explaining the misunderstanding over Clark and praising the Gilpin Players by way of urging Hurston to approve the planned production (MB 214–15). The second letter, to Van Vechten, recounted the two phone calls and asked for Van Vechten's help in getting Hurston to agree to the Cleveland production. Hughes proposed that they should use the versions of Acts I and III that they had written together the previous spring, with Hurston's Act II, but he would clean up the script to make all the parts work well together (MB 218–20). Finally, he sent this version of the play to be copyrighted in both authors' names.

Meanwhile, Hurston had written the promised letter to Hughes. She made the dramatic claim that her work was being "hi-jacked." In Hurston's view, Hughes, out of a presumed romantic attachment to Louise Thompson, had been ready to give her a third of their royalties when she had contributed nothing more than typing. Now, if Langston wanted to give away his own work that way, it was up to him, wrote Hurston, but in making such a proposal about *Mule Bone* he was also giving away her work. The proposal that Louise instead be made the business manager of any Broadway production was even more ludicrous. Why would she want an inexperienced business manager? In that environment, she claimed, there was obviously no way she was going to be treated fairly. Feeling that Louise and Langston were ganging up against her, she had taken her work and left town.

When she returned in the fall, Hurston continued, she had wanted to explain to him how she felt, but was never able to bring herself to do so because she was still too upset. She claimed that she would not have minded sharing the credit and the money with Langston originally, even though the play was based on her own story and she provided the dialogue, but she had had to go her own way when she saw that he was taking advantage of their friendship in order to benefit someone else. She had not wanted to risk saying something in her anger that might lead to the loss of Langston's friendship, but now she was reaching out to him in all sincerity. She reiterated that she knew nothing of the Gilpin Players or Mr. French (mistaking the name of the agency for the name of the agent). What she did not address is that she had had the play copyrighted in her name, but under a different title, the previous October.

Although the general tone of the letter is not angry but rather that of someone wanting to make herself understood, there are places where the tone is more ominous. Near the end of the letter Hurston insists that she has written the play alone and has told Godmother so, as if warning Hughes that power and money are on her side and that this incident could seal his break with Godmother. She also insists in a postscript that both versions of the play are hers and that she never really used any of his suggestions (MB 211–14).

As both Rampersad and Hurston's biographer Robert E. Hemenway suggest, this letter helps to explain Hurston's actions the previous summer and may also offer some insight into Hughes's mysterious breakup with Godmother, which is hardly satisfactorily explained by the dispute over "keeping accounts" and the pressure on Hughes to publish. Their relationship had survived similar stresses and Hughes had been abject enough in his letters, so why hadn't she taken him back this time?

Hurston was clearly jealous of Thompson's relationship with Hughes, though not in an obviously sexual way. Although Hurston denied any romantic interest in Hughes, telling him it made no difference to her whom he loved or wanted to marry, she leaves no doubt that she thinks he is smitten by Thompson and thus is sacrificing Hurston's interests. No evidence supports the idea that Hughes and Thompson were ever more than close friends, but it was an important relationship for Hughes. Hemenway suggests that being a "talented, brilliant woman [Thompson] undoubtedly made suggestions as they dictated, which Hughes at least appreciated. Hurston, seeing her as both a personal and an artistic rival, probably did not" (MB 174–75). Her anger over having Louise intrude on her friendship and her long-anticipated collaboration with Hughes led her to cut off the collaboration and, in her own mind at least, to rewrite the play so as to eliminate anything he had contributed (Hemenway, *MB* 164). But did she go farther?

Rampersad believes that Hurston may have tried to get Thompson fired by complaining to Mason that she and Langston were having an affair, going off together to Hughes's rooms, and leaving Hurston to work on the play alone. Certainly she did make such claims in January 1931 according to Mason's notes (qtd. in *LLH* I: 196), but might she have also made them earlier? Rampersad suggests that she may have gone to Godmother with this story in the summer of 1930, perhaps before going south or perhaps just after her return. Mason's anger over this information could explain both the mysterious firing of Louise and her refusal to be reconciled with Langston.[2]

Rampersad believes Thompson was Hurston's real target. Perhaps she hoped to remove Thompson and then resume work with Hughes. However, Mason responded by banishing Hughes first, "frighten[ing] Hurston into not only shunning his company but also denying that they had ever collaborated" on the play (*LLH* I:196). Whether or not Hurston was responsible for having Thompson fired, Hemenway agrees with Rampersad that part of the reason she kept her distance from Hughes after their initial rupture was her determination to stay in Mason's good graces once she realized Hughes might be permanently out of favor (165).

A third possible motive for Hurston's actions in addition to jealousy of Thompson and the desire to secure her alliance with Mason is professional rivalry with Hughes. Ralph D. Story views the fight over *Mule Bone* as part of the general "literary infighting for recognition and publication" that characterized the Harlem Renaissance. He also notes that Hurston felt that since she had grown up in Eatonville among people like those in the play, she was more qualified than Hughes to tell their story (130, 137). Although Hurston had written to Hughes that she depended on his talent to guide her and that he was "the brains" of their collaboration (qtd. in *LLH* I: 182–83), perhaps this was just flattery to secure his involvement. She expected to remain the senior partner in their collaboration. When he jumped in too eagerly, proposed major plot changes such as making the dispute revolve around a woman rather than a turkey and quickly began thinking of the play as their project rather than hers, Hurston probably felt resentful, even though she had initially solicited his involvement. She may have exaggerated her resentment of Thompson in her letter to Hughes because it was easier to blame a third person than to admit her second thoughts about their collaboration. In turn, she insisted to Mason that Hughes had not contributed anything to the play in part because this was what she thought Mason wanted to hear, but also because this was what she wished were still true.

Whatever the case, Hurston was initially furious over Langston's insistence that he was co-author of the "revised" play and did not hesitate to give Godmother her side of the story. As late as the morning of January 20 she was reiterating her complaint that Langston was trying to make a claim to some of her royalties just because she had discussed the play with him (MB 225–26). But given her mixed motives, Hurston's tune changed depending on her audience. To Van Vechten she sobbed that she cared deeply for Langston and was distraught about the whole "misunderstanding" (MB 223). Initially she apparently instructed the Samuel French agency to refuse permission to the Gilpin Players to do the play. A telegram for Rowena Jelliffe arrived to that effect on January 20. But later that day, Hurston was appeased by a persuasive phone call from the representatives of the *Cleveland Plain Dealer,* which was sponsoring the production. She agreed to come supervise the rehearsals and to authorize the performance if all went to her satisfaction. Over the next 24 hours she sent three additional telegrams herself, giving permission to proceed but also trying to maintain control by insisting that only she could authorize any changes to the script (MB 225).

Reassured to learn that Hughes had nothing to do with the manuscript arriving in Cleveland and encouraged by the tone of the letter he wrote her on January 19, Hurston wrote a friendly letter to Hughes on January 20 after her conversation with the sponsors. In it, she suggested that maybe both of them had overreacted and promised to write to Godmother on his behalf. She kept this promise, sending a second letter to Mason on the night of January 20, informing her that Langston was not after all, responsible for offering the play to Gilpin Players. She did not concede that he had contributed anything to her play, but suggested that since Langston was a "weak" person, he had probably been persuaded by other parties to try to take advantage of his relationship to Zora and stake a claim to some of the royalties. Leaving herself room to come to an agreement with Hughes without admitting that he was her collaborator, she confided that she felt so relieved and happy that Langston had decided to be "honorable" that she might even give him part of the credit and royalties for the play (MB 226–28).

She would not feel this way for long. Hughes was so annoyed when he received Hurston's first letter that he immediately wrote an intemperate reply (dated January 20), which crossed in the mail with her conciliatory response. First, he claimed that Hurston's position about Louise was "ab-

surd" since Hurston knew perfectly well that once they were able to pay
Thompson for the typing with Mason's funds she had no further claim on
the play. Hughes's own claim was another matter. He pointed out that one
of the versions of the play that had been sent out under her name was a
carbon copy of the work they had done together. Of course the play was
partially his. He was willing to consider giving her a greater share of the
royalties, but if she tried to deny his rights, he would sue. He begged her
not to let the dispute make them lose the opportunity to finish the play
and have it produced in Cleveland (MB 220–22).

Hughes also attempted to call Arthur Spingarn long-distance in order
to get legal advice, but was not able to reach him right away. By the time
he did get in touch, late on the evening of January 20—just about the
time that Hurston was telling Godmother that maybe Langston wasn't as
awful as she had thought—Rowena Jelliffe had received the telegrams
that seemed to authorize the Cleveland production and Hughes was no
longer sure that any legal action was necessary. But he agreed to write to
his lawyer with details of the whole story the next day.

In his long letter dated January 21, Hughes reviewed what had hap-
pened so far and explained that the Gilpin Players had started rehearsing
the play in anticipation of Hurston's arrival on February 1. He gave a list
of evidence and witnesses who could attest to his role in the writing of the
play. Hughes told Spingarn that he believed that Hurston would agree to
collaborate with him again, but he was anxious to get an official agreement signed between the two of them and the Gilpin Players, as well as a
personal agreement between himself and Hurston over how the royalties
would be split. He repeated the proposal he made to Hurston the day before that he would accept one-third of the royalties with two-thirds going
to Hurston, in the interest of seeing the play go on. He asked Spingarn to
negotiate with Hurston on his behalf (MB 229–39).

On January 22, believing that everything had been worked out,
Hughes addressed a cheery letter to "Zora, my darling." After flattering
her and telling her that the Jelliffes were eager to meet her after all the
good things he had been telling them about her, he got down to business.
He asked her to get in touch with Spingarn to formalize the one-
third/two-thirds split of the royalties and asked for permission to represent
her interests as well as his own in negotiating royalties with the Gilpin
Players who wanted a signed agreement as soon as possible. On January
24, he wrote to Spingarn that everything was going smoothly. Hurston
was expected on February 1 and in the meantime, he offered details of two
different royalty proposals offered by the Gilpin Players and asked Spingarn to present them to Hurston.

However the very day that Hughes wrote this optimistic letter, Spingarn was facing an irate Hurston in his office. What Hughes had not taken into account was how angry his letter of January 20 would make Hurston, who went back to insisting that Hughes had no part in the creation of the play. After breaking an appointment with Spingarn on Friday, January 23, she came to his office on Saturday morning and accused Hughes of lying about his contributions to the play. Spingarn suggested to Hughes that his threat of litigation in the January 20 letter had been ill advised and that he and Hurston should try to work things out in a face-to-face meeting. Meanwhile, he informed Hughes that Hurston was still not sure whether she wanted a Cleveland production of her play and needed to talk to her agent, Elizabeth Marbury, before making any decision (MB 244–45).

On January 26, Marbury wrote Rowena Jelliffe on Hurston's behalf, proposing that the Gilpin Players pay Zora's fare to Cleveland in lieu of royalties. Jelliffe showed the letter to Hughes who wrote to Marbury that he was part-author of the play. Jelliffe agreed to pay the fare in *addition* to the royalties and Spingarn informed Hughes that Hurston wanted to talk to him face-to-face about the royalty question, which he believed was for the best. Spingarn also mentioned in passing that Locke had been in to see him and had spoken on Hurston's behalf.

This information upset Hughes greatly, especially when Locke replied flippantly to a telegram from Hughes asking him to explain his statements to Spingarn. He began to fear that Hurston was going to insist that the play was hers alone even after coming to Cleveland and would perhaps convince everyone else to believe her. His fears intensified after Jelliffe received a letter from Paul Banks, a member of the Gilpin Players, who was in New York and had called on Hurston. Banks reported that Hurston not only told him that Hughes was lying about his contributions to the play but that Spingarn himself had become convinced of Hughes's dishonesty and was no longer willing to represent him. According to Banks, Hurston was coming to Cleveland to supervise the performance of her own play and would insist that Hughes have no connection with the production (MB 255). When Spingarn received a troubled letter from Hughes regarding the accusations of Banks, he replied soothingly that Hurston was distorting his words. He had not claimed he would refuse to represent Hughes but urged her not to look at the situation as a legal matter at present, but rather a dispute that could be settled amicably. He reassured Hughes that he believed in his honesty and had defended him to Hurston and had also urged her to settle the matter rather than giving up on the play as Hurston had threatened to do. Striking an optimistic note, he again predicted that the matter would be easily resolved once the writers met in person.

According to the account Hughes later gave Spingarn, for a time this optimism seemed justified. Although Hurston's dealings with the Gilpin Players got off to a rocky start when she failed to show up for a scheduled meeting on Sunday, February 1, the group agreed to reconsider their decision to cancel the play when Hurston presented herself on Monday, February 2. First Hurston and Hughes met alone to iron out their differences. Hurston apparently repeated her grievances about Thompson and her claim to have rewritten the play after breaking off with Hughes. Hughes countered that the matter of Thompson's compensation had long been settled, and pointed to similarities between the revision and the script on which they had collaborated. After Hughes agreed that Hurston's name would be listed first, she agreed that the play could be offered to the Gilpin Players as their joint work. They then met with Jelliffe and Elmer Cheeks, the president of the Gilpin Players, who agreed to call a meeting for Tuesday night at which the troupe would vote on whether or not to go forward with the play.

Before this meeting took place, Hurston apparently changed her mind again. She telephoned Jelliffe in a rage, claiming that Jelliffe had acted unfairly by taking Hughes's side before she had ever contacted Hurston. Since Hughes had come down with an acute attack of tonsillitis, Jelliffe invited Hurston to come to a meeting at Hughes's bedside. Those present, besides Hughes, Hurston, and Jelliffe, were Hughes's mother, Jelliffe's husband, and a "Mr. Banks," who accompanied Hurston, perhaps the same man who had taken her side after meeting her in New York. Hurston was furious and was verbally abusive to both Hughes and Jelliffe and again brought up her anger over Thompson's role. Carrie Clark defended her son, refusing to let Hurston have the last word. In a telegram to Godmother, however, Hurston claimed that it was she who had triumphed by putting a stop to Hughes and Thompson's attempt to steal her play (*LLH* I: 198).

While Hughes presents Hurston's change of heart as inexplicable in his letter to Spingarn, in *The Big Sea*, he claims that her anger was in response to learning that Thompson had been in town and had spoken to the Jelliffes in support of Hughes's authorship earlier in the month (333). Hughes may not have wanted to embarrass Louise (whom he does not name in the *Big Sea*) by identifying her to Spingarn, or he may have been genuinely puzzled by Hurston's actions, suspecting that her public anger at Thompson covered other motivations. Perhaps in their face-to-face meeting, Hurston had felt unable to resist Hughes's appeals, but once alone her resentments resurfaced. Or, she could have become frightened over how she would explain to Godmother her decision to let Hughes be listed as co-author on a play to which she insisted he had contributed nothing.

With Hurston's angry departure there was no more chance of a Cleveland production of the play and little prospect that she would ever change her mind. Nevertheless, Hughes wrote Spingarn that if she ever did agree to collaborate, he would be ready to resume work. Meanwhile he was prepared to challenge any attempt by Hurston to sell the play as her own (MB 263). About a month later, Hurston went to Spingarn's office and proposed that she would eliminate all parts of the play to which Langston claimed to have contributed and then sell the play under her name (MB 267). Hughes indicated that he might be agreeable to this solution, but within two weeks Hurston was again angrily denying that Hughes had any claim to any part of the play, accusing Hughes (to both Mason and Spingarn) of making a copy of her script while he was in Cleveland and then claiming they had written it together (MB 270–71). With the dispute unresolved, the play was never performed or published in Hurston's lifetime, though the third act would be published, with the consent of Hughes, in 1964.

Sixty years after the play was abandoned it was finally performed on Broadway by Lincoln Center Theater in February 1991. The production coincided with the publication of an edition of the text prepared by Hughes's literary executor George Houston Bass—who also wrote a prologue for the play—and Henry Louis Gates, Jr. The production itself received mostly negative reviews. As Patrick Pacheco pointed out, characters originally conceived as a corrective to the "darky" stereotypes that then populated the stages of Broadway and vaudeville may themselves seem like dated caricatures to modern audiences. Yet he observed that the play retained an authentic quality to which black audiences responded, despite some changes to accommodate notions of political correctness (4). Frank Rich, on the other hand, disparaged the production as "watered down" and "Disneyesque." For him the production showed *Mule Bone* to be "a false start that remains one of the American theaters more tantalizing might-have-beens" (1).

Notes

1. A letter from Hughes to Carl Van Vechten on January 19 places the call on the previous evening. We know it took place no later than January 18 because in a postscript to a letter also dated January 18, Hurston refers to the phone call as having already taken

place. In a letter from Hughes to Arthur Spingarn on January 21, Hughes claims to have gotten in touch with Hurston "at once," leading Henry Louis Gates to suggest January 16 as the evening of the call (*MB* 12). Robert E. Hemenway, Hurston's biographer, also places the call on January 16 (*MB* 167) but Rampersad dates it on January 17 (*LLH* I: 195).

2. That Thompson was fired does not really seem surprising since she would not have had much typing to do with Hughes at Hedgerow and Hurston out of touch. What is un-explained is Mrs. Mason's anger at Thompson.

Chapter 10

A TURN TOWARD SOCIALISM

While the *Mule Bone* crisis was unraveling, Hughes did get one piece of good news. Locke had nominated *Not Without Laughter* for the Harmon medal, an annual prize in many categories for achievement by blacks, and Hughes won the medal for literature in 1930. More important for Hughes, the award carried a prize of $400, which made possible an escape. His thoughts turned again to Cuba and to Haiti, as well. Hughes had long revered Haiti as the site of the first independent black republic and still hoped to make it the subject of an opera. Since his previous visit to Cuba many young black writers throughout the Caribbean had become interested in Hughes's work and looked to him as a leader of a literary movement that emphasized racial pride and the need to shake off the effects of colonialism.

This time Hughes would not travel alone, or by cruise liner. A new acquaintance, a young, black artist named Zell Ingram, agreed to drive Hughes down to Florida in his mother's car. After finishing the play *Mulatto* and finally undergoing a tonsillectomy, Hughes headed south with Ingram. They made the trip uneventfully in six days, took a train from Miami to Key West and then a boat to Havana, traveling second class. The small crowd that welcomed them at the dock included Nicolás Guillén and two other writers Hughes had met on his previous visit and a photographer and representative from *Orbe*, a weekly magazine now edited by José Fernández de Castro, which featured pictures and a story about Hughes's visit in the next issue.

Hughes spent about two weeks in Cuba, which, as he recounts in the second volume of his autobiography, *I Wonder as I Wander*, were marred by an incident that illustrated the force of the "color line" in Cuba despite the appearance of being a more integrated society. José Fernández de Castro had invited Hughes and Ingram to a party at Havana Beach one evening. The two Americans decided to go to the beach in the afternoon and spend the whole day there, but the attendant refused to sell them admission tickets. Hughes and Ingram discovered that while the beach charged its posted dollar daily admission to whites (often American tourists), it had an unofficial policy of requiring darker skinned patrons to purchase a season pass. Such passes cost ten times the daily rate and were sold only to those colored residents who had "enough political pull or social prestige to *force* the management" to sell the ticket (*IW* 12). Hughes asked to speak to the manager but the attendant called a bouncer instead. Ingram was ready to fight at this point, but Hughes calmed him and suggested they go into the lobby and call Fernández de Castro to intervene.

As soon as they sat down in the lobby after placing the call, a policeman approached who had been called by the bouncer. The policeman informed them that the manager wanted them to leave. Hughes again demanded to speak to the manager. The manager came over, accompanied by four more armed policemen who escorted the two Americans back to the streetcar platform outside the entrance to the beach.

Annoyed that they remained there, the bouncer tried to make them move off but was intimidated by the threat of Ingram's fists. He called the police again and soon a wail of sirens heralded the arrival of a police van. Hughes and Ingram were hustled into the van and driven to the police station where the captain treated them respectfully, recording the charges but refusing to put them in a cell. When Fernández de Castro arrived, they were released and told to report for a hearing the next morning.

Hughes and Ingram told their story at the hearing but were refuted by witnesses for the hotel who offered fraudulent testimony. These witnesses accused them of entering the lobby with wet bathing suits and annoying other guests with boorish behavior, thus requiring forcible eviction. The judge pointed out that this testimony was inconsistent with the arrest of the two in street clothes on the platform outside the hotel and dismissed the charges with apologies to the visitors.

Visiting Haiti was the real goal of Langston's trip. After a week's stay in Port-au-Prince, the travelers made a pilgrimage to the Citadel at Cap Haïtien. They squeezed into a bus where 8 to 10 passengers were crammed into seats built for six. The roof and floors were packed with luggage—including chickens and pigs—and the bus had open sides. They expected a trip of about 12 hours, but a road was washed out at St. Marc about halfway across the island. Although the bus turned around, Hughes and

Ingram elected to get off in St. Marc where they waited three weeks for the waters to subside and the road to be repaired. They then climbed into an even more overcrowded bus to continue their journey, only to have the bus run out of gas at nightfall. They were high in the hills, far from any town, and it was well after sunrise before a peasant returned with a can of gasoline. Ingram spent the night huddling amid the baggage on top the bus, while Hughes took refuge in an empty pipe near the roadside. The next day brought a torrential downpour, which drenched the passengers as it blew in the open sides of the bus, but they finally reached Cap Haïtien.

At their hotel, the two Americans quickly attracted the interest of two young women. Coloma, from Santo Domingo, soon captivated Ingram, while her friend Clezie-Anne became devoted to Hughes and taught him some of the local patois, for his Parisian French was not understood by most of the people.

The hotel was comfortable and charged only $25 a month, but Ingram and Hughes sometimes sought to supplement the hotel's monotonous fare of fish, rice, and plantains with supplies purchased in the general store. The hotel manager had no objection to their having the cook prepare these extra delicacies, but objected strenuously to their carrying their purchases home themselves. He explained that gentlemen in Haiti must never carry parcels. It was a mark of class distinction like wearing shoes and a jacket. He also chided his guests for spending too much time talking with the common people and offered to introduce them to people of the higher classes. However, Hughes was enjoying the time spent with the people who owned no shoes, and had indeed made a conscious decision not to use his letters of introduction to the elite of Haiti. Hughes questioned whether the emphasis on coats and shoes might be "carried over from the long ago days of the white masters, who wore coats and shoes— and had force and power" (*IW* 28). Even though Hughes's light skin and education suggested to the hotel owner that he belonged to the upper classes, Langston found himself drawn to the exploited dark-skinned laborers.

While in Haiti, Hughes answered one letter that he had been carrying around since January. His father had read *Not Without Laughter* and wrote to say that he enjoyed the book, though not Hughes's extensive use of dialect. He asked Langston whether he was actually able to make a living as a writer (*LLH* I: 208). Hughes claimed that he had been able to survive on his writings, but that was only true if one counts the money he had received from patrons, especially Mason. For most of his life Hughes had had various other jobs to make ends meet. Knowing that he would be returning to a depression in which "scholarships and literary prizes" would be increasingly difficult to come by and even competition for work as a busboy or messman would be more keen, Hughes "began to puzzle out how, I, a *Negro*, could make a living in America from writing," when the jobs that traditionally supported writers such as editorial jobs in publishing houses or with magazines were generally closed to blacks (*IW* 4).

To save money, since the supply from the Harmon award was running low after nearly four months, Ingram and Hughes decided to take deck passage on a Dutch boat bound for Cuba. It stopped for one day in Port-au-Prince and Hughes reluctantly donned both coat and shoes in order to go and call on the poet Jacques Roumain. He spent a pleasant hour with the poet and his wife. Roumain was sorry to hear that Hughes was leaving that night and could not be introduced to other writers and government officials. After meeting Roumain, Hughes purchased food for the journey and returned to the boat. When he reached it, he was hot and tired and stripped off most of his clothes. He and Ingram spread out a newspaper and began to make a meal from the sausages, bananas, cheese, bread, and wine Hughes had purchased. In the middle of this undignified meal, a delegation led by Roumain arrived unexpectedly to make speeches of welcome and farewell and to offer him baskets of fruit, rum, and other local gifts.

If this Haitian delegation were surprised to see their distinguished visitors traveling on the open deck, the immigration officials at Santiago, Cuba, where the Dutch vessel next docked, were no less incredulous. They assumed that the two men were sugar cane workers and detained them for three days until the American Consul had them released with instructions to take immediate passage for Florida. However, it was necessary to spend the night in a hotel in Havana, and when it came time to get up the next morning, Ingram was too ill to rise from the mattress. Misdiagnosed as having malaria, Ingram actually recovered in a couple of days and the two finally sailed for Key West.

In Miami, Ingram's car proved to have flat tires, and they had to pawn most of their possessions to get new tires and pay the bill for parking the car for all those months. Hughes did have a little money in the bank in New York, but no way to access it, until he thought of Mary McLeod Bethune. Hughes and Ingram had spent the night at Bethune-Cookman College at Daytona Beach on their way down to Miami, and had been received very warmly by Bethune, the founder and president. Now Hughes hoped that she might cash his check, giving them much needed traveling money.

She did even more, proposing that as she was planning to go north anyway, she could ride up with Hughes and Ingram. Although the car was barely large enough for three passengers, Bethune's presence meant that people were eager to offer the travelers a bed for the night and plenty of food. As Hughes explained, "Mrs. Bethune...was known far and wide at conclaves, conventions and church meetings. She had spoken at every colored school in the South, too. People loved her, so they showed it by offering her their best" (IW 40).

Occasionally, Bethune would suggest that Hughes read a few poems to their hosts, introducing Hughes as a poet that the South should know better. She repeatedly encouraged him to undertake a reading tour of the South. After returning to New York in August, Hughes began to contemplate Bethune's suggestion seriously. He made lists of the heads of Negro schools in the South and wrote to gauge their interest in having him read at their schools. He applied to the Rosenwald Fund to support his project, seeking funding for an automobile so that he would not have to rely on segregated public transportation and would be free to travel in rural areas far from the railroad lines. The fund contributed $1,000, of which about $600 went for the purchase of a new Model A Ford. Since Hughes did not know how to drive, he hired W. Radcliffe Lewis, who had been his classmate at Lincoln, to be both his chauffer and business manager in exchange for 40 percent of the profits.

He remained in New York for three months before embarking on the tour, living once again at the YMCA in Harlem where he had stayed upon his arrival from Mexico ten years earlier. During this time, Hughes was writing and publishing radical verse, prose, and drama including "A Letter from Haiti" and "People Without Shoes," both inspired by his time in Haiti; the long poem "Advertisement for the Waldorf-Astoria," which juxtaposed actual advertising copy for the new luxury hotel with the plight of the "homeless and hungry ones" who were advised to "choose the Waldorf as a background for your rags" (CP 143–46); and several pieces about the Scottsboro incident.

In March 1931 in Alabama, a white mob accompanied by two armed policemen pulled nine black teenagers, aged 12 to 19 years, from a freight train on which they had been riding illegally. The raid on the train had followed a fistfight between some of the blacks and four white men who had also been riding the train illegally. Three of the white men were forced off the train as a result of the fight, and they complained to the stationmaster at Stevenson, Alabama, that they had been attacked by a gang of blacks. The stationmaster wired the news to the next stop at Paint Rock, Alabama, and an armed white mob met the train. Two white women, mill workers named Victoria Price and Ruby Bates, were also riding the train. When discovered and questioned during the raid on the train in Paint Rock, the women claimed that they had been gang-raped by as many as 12 armed blacks after the whites left the train. The black youths were then all accused of rape, even though some were riding in cars far from the scene of the fight or the alleged rapes. They were bound, taken to the jail in Scottsboro, and nearly lynched by a mob that approached the jail that night, but the National Guard thwarted the lynchers. The Scottsboro boys, as they came to be called, were assigned incompetent counsel and put on trial only 12 days later amid inflammatory newspaper coverage that presumed the boys' guilt. While six of the boys proclaimed their innocence, others were beaten into testifying that some of the other defendants had raped the women. The defendants were tried in three groups before all-white juries. The trials ended with eight of the accused sentenced to the electric chair and one mistrial in the case of the youngest defendant, Roy Williams, when one of the 12 jurors held out for a life sentence rather than the death penalty.

In the summer and fall of 1931, the papers were full of the case. Fearing a political backlash, the NAACP had hesitated to get involved. The Communist Party took up the case through its International Labor Defense organization (ILD), seeing it as an opportunity to recruit American blacks. The ILD eventually took charge of the appeal over the objections of the NAACP. This brought the party new prestige and respect among American blacks, including Hughes. His sympathies with radical politics were reflected in poems like "Union" which called for the poor, both white and black, to unite against greed, and "Open Letter to the South" in which the speaker is the black worker who offers the white worker his hand so that together they can "[break] the time clock, [smash] misery" and take control of "tools and banks and mines / Railroads, ships and dams" (CP 160–61). These sympathies were also explicit in "Scottsboro, Limited: A One Act Play" which ends with "Red voices" that urge the condemned black boys to fight back, inspiring them to destroy the electric chair and unite with the white workers.

Hughes knew that these works would not endear him to the audience he sought on his reading tour, and not all the verse he wrote in 1931–32 was radical. Hughes also wrote a long poem called "The Negro Mother," a dramatic monologue in which the title character tells "of the long dark way / That I had to climb, that I had to know / in order that I might live and grow" (CP 155–56). This poem, together with five others, formed the content of an inexpensive booklet that Hughes proposed to sell on the tour. The booklet, entitled *"The Negro Mother" and Other Dramatic Recitations* was illustrated by a white artist, Prentiss Taylor, and published by Golden Stair Press in the fall of 1931 in time for the tour. Golden Stair

Press printed posters and broadsides for the tour, as well. Hughes also persuaded Knopf to publish a one-dollar edition of *The Weary Blues*. He hoped that sales of these items would supplement his speaking fees.

These fees were flexible. Officially he charged $50 for a reading but since many of the schools were too poor to afford this rate, he charged as little as $10 or offered to give a free program in exchange for a place to sleep and the opportunity to sell his books. He later recalled, "No matter how small a dot on a map a town was, we did not scorn it, and my audiences ranged all the way from college students to cotton pickers, from kindergarten children to the inmates of old folks homes" (*IW* 55). According to Rampersad, he began his program with an autobiographical emphasis, reading some of his lighter poems and tying them to his life experiences. Next there would usually be a performance by local musicians, followed by Hughes reading a second set of poems with more serious themes. Hughes closed with the poem "I, Too" (*LLH* I: 223). For the most part, Hughes charmed his audiences and was in turn charmed by them. In a report Hughes sent to the Rosenwald Foundation in March 1932 he declared that he had come to know the South for the first time and that he was convinced that his poetry was meaningful to even his uneducated audiences. By this time he had given 54 readings and earned $1,337.83 from fees and sales of his pamphlets (*LLH* I: 233).

Yet there were unpleasant incidents as well. Soon after the tour began, Hughes read at the Hampton Institute on the same weekend that two tragic incidents occurred. A former Hampton athlete who was now a football coach at a black college in Alabama was beaten to death in Birmingham for parking his car in a lot designated for whites. Meanwhile Juliette Derricote, an educator and official of the YWCA, died of her injuries following a car accident after a white hospital refused to admit her. The students at Hampton wanted to plan a protest and Hughes was eager to be involved, but the dean refused to allow it, claiming that the Institute's purpose was education, not activism. Hughes was stunned by this attitude and to find throughout the South that administrators at many black colleges were unwilling to confront racial injustice or take a stand on the Scottsboro case or other issues.

At the only white university where Hughes read, the University of North Carolina at Chapel Hill, police stood guard outside while he gave his reading. Many whites were incensed over two controversial pieces related to the Scottsboro incident that were published in *Contempo*, an unofficial student publication, on the day of his scheduled lecture. Hughes had sent the poem "Christ in Alabama" and the essay "Southern Gentlemen, White Prostitutes, Mill-Owners and Negroes" at the request of the editors of *Contempo*. Though some readers wanted him run out of town, the university refused to cancel the reading and Hughes probably benefited from the publicity.

In Nashville, following a triumphant reading at Fisk University where he was introduced by James Weldon Johnson, Hughes and Johnson had been invited to attend a party hosted by Thomas Mabry, an English instructor at Vanderbilt. But the critic Allen Tate refused to attend the party and successfully pressured Mabry to cancel it. Tate claimed that, while he admired Hughes and Johnson as writers and would have been willing to meet them in the North, he was unwilling to defy Southern custom to meet socially with blacks. Hughes had a similar experience at the home of Julia Peterkin, a white author on black subjects who had met Hughes in the North and invited him to call on her. When Hughes was reading in South Carolina, he attempted to visit her plantation only to be rudely dismissed by a man on her porch who repeatedly insisted that Peterkin was not at home.

In general, the tour made Hughes more acutely aware of the social and cultural gaps between blacks and whites in the South and the disheartening lack of protest against the situation, especially among so-called Negro leaders. He wrote contemptuously of them in poems like "Ph.D." and "To Certain Negro Leaders" (CP 161; 136), and he continued to include poems on issues like lynching and the Scottsboro case in his readings. Although he was dissuaded from seeking an interview with Ruby Bates, he did visit the Scottsboro boys on Death Row in a Montgomery prison, but they offered little response when he read some of his poetry to them.

While on tour he managed a visit with his old friend, Arna Bontemps, who was then teaching at Oakwood Junior College near Huntswood, Alabama. During his visit he and Bontemps made plans to collaborate on a children's book about a Haitian brother and sister that would be called *Popo and Fifina*. Bontemps handled the negotiations with his publisher, Macmillan, securing a $150 advance for each author.

Hughes was also involved in another juvenile project, a book of verse for children called *The Dream Keeper*. In late March he interrupted his tour for a brief visit to New York City. During the visit he met with Prentiss Taylor to discuss another Golden Stair Press project. Hughes's play *Scottsboro Limited*, and four related poems would appear together with illustrations by Taylor. Hughes also visited the Knopf office to approve the illustrations for *The Dream Keeper* and spoke to Louise Thompson about an intriguing project. Thompson was in charge of recruiting black performers willing to travel to the Soviet Union at their own expense in order to participate in the making of a film about race relations in the

United States. The performers were to be reimbursed, but having to pay their own way initially was a deterrent to persuading actors to volunteer. Thompson asked Hughes to help her recruit, and he consented. He also agreed to consider traveling to Russia himself and helping to write the script.

Hughes resumed his tour with a new driver, George Lee, and an unpaid personal secretary, James Ronald Derry. Both Lee and Derry were former Lincoln University students. The group traveled through Texas and then headed for California. In Los Angeles, Hughes was housed at the home of Loren Miller, a newspaper columnist who often spoke on the cause of radical socialism. Miller belonged to the local John Reed Club and had wanted to put on Hughes's play *Scottsboro Limited*, but had been stopped by the police, who feared a public disturbance. However Hughes did deliver a lecture to the club and on May 8, his play was produced in Los Angeles as part of a mass meeting on the Scottsboro issue. Hughes also traveled with Miller to see the Boulder Dam construction site where they queried officials about why no blacks had been hired for the project.

Thompson wired Hughes that the Soviet production company was ready to get started on the film project and both Hughes and Loren Miller agreed to sail for Russia in June.

Hughes began to wind up his tour with readings in northern California, Oregon, and Washington. In San Francisco, he had been invited to stay at the home of Noël Sullivan, a wealthy white man who supported various liberal causes. Hughes was welcomed warmly into Sullivan's household, and another important friendship began.

Hughes returned to New York on June 14, just in time to board the *Europa* as it sailed for Germany, taking Hughes and 21 others on their way to Moscow. Although it would not turn out the way that he planned, his experience in the Soviet Union would be very significant in his life and art.

Chapter 11

FILM PROJECT IN MOSCOW

Given the political direction of his recent poetry, and his admiration of the Communist response to the Scottsboro incident, Hughes could only be thrilled with the prospect of visiting the Soviet Union. He idealized it as a utopia where both economic exploitation and racial prejudice had been eradicated. Aside from Hughes, only a few of the 22 young people who joined the expedition had done so out of a commitment to radical politics. These included Louise Thompson, Loren Miller, and Alan McKenzie (who was the only Communist Party member). Nor were many serious about filmmaking. Since few seasoned performers would seriously consider paying their own way to Russia to work on an ill-defined project for which no contract or script was available ahead of time, Thompson had not had the luxury of being selective. Only Sylvia Garner and Wayland Rudd were experienced actors, and there was one singer, two creative writers (Hughes and Dorothy West), and two journalists. Many were college students or recent graduates who had simply joined the group in the spirit of adventure.

The film was actually to be made under the auspices of a German company called Meschrabpohm Films; its parent company was the Workers International Relief Fund, based in Berlin. The group was stranded in Berlin briefly because their visas for the Soviet Union had not been pre-arranged as they had supposed. Then they took a train to the Baltic coast, a ship to Helsinki, and another train to Leningrad where they were welcomed as representatives of "the downtrodden Negro workers of America" (*LLH* I: 244).

After a tour of Leningrad the group moved on to Moscow, where they were housed in the Grand Hotel. As promised, Meschrabpohm Films refunded everyone's travel costs in U.S. dollars. They signed contracts that promised 400 rubles a month for four months to be actors in the movie, a generous salary by Moscow standards. Hughes, who was to work on the script, was offered slightly more and was pleased with the terms, though he had to insist that his contract be translated into English before he signed. The proposed script that Hughes was to modify, as necessary, was also written in Russian. Thus, for the first few weeks the group members were free to enjoy themselves while they waited for a translation. Despite facing minor hardships in terms of the scarcity of fresh vegetables and items like toilet paper, the Americans lived well and were treated very deferentially by the people of Moscow, who called them "Negro comrades" and offered them their seats on public transportation or invited them ahead in line. The group was often invited to parties and theatrical performances and introduced to great performers as if they were all distinguished actors as well.

Finally Hughes received the translated script for the film, entitled *Black and White*. Hughes read it eagerly but found it unusable. The writer had never been to the United States, and the resulting script was completely implausible. Set in Birmingham, Alabama, the story concerned the exploitation of blacks as mill workers and servants in the homes of the rich, white bosses and owners. The film would dramatize a conflict in which a labor organizer struggles to unite both black and white workers while the capitalists who own the mills seek to turn the white workers against the blacks to prevent unionization. Hughes conceded that the basic story was "ideologically correct," but protested such elements as a scene in which a wealthy white man dances with his black maid at a party, a plot premise in which wealthy blacks in Birmingham own their own radio stations, and a climatic riot scene in which unionized white workers from the North come to the aid of the black workers against the poor whites of the South, who have been duped by the capitalists into turning on the blacks. He at last convinced those in charge of the film that the screenplay needed to be completely rewritten. Hughes declined to take on that job, alleging his ignorance of steel mills, unions, and the South itself, and so the German director of the film, Karl Junghans, agreed to try. Meanwhile, the cast began to rehearse the musical numbers. This only brought further consternation, since few of them could sing. Junghans was also concerned that the group could not give convincing portrayals of black workers in screen tests. They were generally too young, too light-skinned and appeared too refined for the roles they were expected to play.

The script problems had pushed back the date of filming considerably to August 15. Morale was low, so in early August the restless young Americans were invited on an excursion to Odessa and a cruise on the Black Sea while waiting for filming to begin. Henry Lee Moon, a member of the group, had been left behind in Moscow because he was ill, but just after the cruise ended he showed up in Odessa with disturbing news. The *Paris Herald Tribune* had published a news article alleging that the *Black and White* project had been abandoned because of a fear that the United States, which was on the verge of recognizing the Soviet Union diplomatically, might resent this scrutiny of its internal affairs and reconsider its decision. The Americans were disappointed to see their dreams of movie stardom vanish and complained bitterly that the press knew of the cancellation before the film company had bothered to inform them. Some charged that the film company and perhaps the Soviet government had betrayed the cause of communism by abandoning an important political film in order to court the favor of a capitalist country.

A Meschrabpohm official arrived the next day and hastened to explain that the film project was not abandoned, only postponed. However, the project would be carried on with a new script and a new group of actors. The present group would still be paid for the remainder of their four-month contracts, and they could choose to leave Moscow immediately, take a tour first and then go home, or settle in Moscow as immigrants. Despite these assurances, most of the Americans were disappointed and angry, especially when they returned to Moscow to find that their hotel rooms had been rented to other guests and their own belongings moved to a cheaper and decidedly inferior hotel. Hughes, by contrast, at least according to his account in *I Wonder as I Wander*, had not felt optimistic about the project since he had first seen the script. He was somewhat relieved to be released from further involvement with what would have been an embarrassingly bad film (*IW* 98).

There was dissension within the group over what to do next. Thompson and Miller wanted to make a reasoned argument in favor of continuing the production with an improved script, while another faction was more interested in hurling accusations of bad faith on the part of the production company and calling attention to the betrayal of the cause of Negro rights. This faction would not concede that there might be any truth to Meschrabpobhm's claims that both the script and the actors were unsuitable for the project they envisioned, and when Hughes defended that argument he was criticized by Ted Poston, another group member, for being an apologist for the Communists (*IW* 98; *LLH* I: 250).

A delegation including Hughes, Miller, Poston, and Moon met with the Comintern to present their arguments. The Comintern was the organization in charge of national communist parties worldwide, and it was headquartered in Moscow. Hughes hoped that the Comintern might at least recognize the importance of the project and affirm a commitment to making a film that would accurately dramatize race relations in the future. Poston and Moon seemed to hope that their denunciations of the film company and the Soviet government for their anti-revolutionary behavior might bring about the censure of the Comintern and force the resumption of the project. The Comintern ultimately supported the decision to postpone the project. About half of the group, including Hughes, then took up Meschrabpobhm's offer of a tour of the Soviet Union. Five members, including Poston and Moon, immediately returned to the United States, while others went to Europe or stayed in Moscow.

The tour, which would depart a month later, was to take them through Central Asia and offer the visitors a view of how racial minorities fared in the Soviet Union. The group already favorably contrasted the treatment they had received in Russia with what they endured back home, and Hughes celebrated the freedom he found as a result of the Communist revolution in several poems. "Good Morning, Revolution" was written toward the end of the summer of 1932. In this poem the speaker welcomes Revolution as a "best friend" who will help him take charge of the "tools of production" for the benefit of the workers, not the bosses. The poem also predicts the spread of revolution around the world (CP 162–63). Hughes sent the poem to the Saturday Evening Post, which rejected it. It was published instead in The New Masses. Rampersad suggests that this rejection prompted a satirical reference to the Post in the poem "Goodbye Christ" which Hughes wrote in September and which would cause much trouble for him in later years (LLH I: 252). In this poem, the speaker attacks organized religion and dismisses Christ as irrelevant to modern concerns. Religious faith has been manipulated for profit and to exploit the masses. The speaker demands that Christ "make way for a new guy with no religion at all— / A real guy named / Marx Communist Lenin Peasant Stalin Worker ME—" (CP 166).

Hughes gave a copy of this poem to Otto Huiswood, a contributing editor for a German magazine, The Negro Worker, who was then in Moscow. Huiswood, without consulting Hughes, sent the poem to the magazine, which published it in the November–December issue. As Walter C. Daniel explains, back in the United States the poem soon provoked a controversy in the black press. In January in the Pittsburgh Courier, the Reverend J. Raymond Henderson published a refutation of what he saw as the main ideas of the poem. It was not true that Christ had had his day, nor was the Bible a fiction, nor was Christ or belief in his teachings impeding the progress of race relations or social justice. In a later issue,

Melvin Tolson, a poet and English professor, responded by defending the poem as "a challenge and a warning to the churches...of the world." The controversy continued through March. Another defender was James Oliver Slade, who argued that in the poem "Christ" stood for the church in the United States, which has allowed itself to be distracted from Christ's philosophy of brotherly love. D. Ormonde Walker argued that the poem was lamenting the failure of religion and of the Church to do enough to "curb man's prejudices." George Schyuler used the discussion of the poem as an occasion to critique the materialism of American churches, both black and white. The last word on the subject to appear in the *Courier* was a parody by Reverdy C. Ransom entitled "All Hail to Christ" which dismisses Hughes instead of Christ and argues that while Christ brought a reign of peace, Lenin and Stalin, Hughes's new saints, are responsible for violence and fear (Daniel 132–34). Although Hughes was still abroad while this controversy took place, a March 1, 1933, letter to Van Vechten from Moscow indicates he was aware of it and confident that the poem had been capably defended (Bernard 101). Nevertheless, the outcry against the poem would resurface with such force in later years that Hughes would be compelled to repudiate the poem.

For now Hughes was happy with the reception given his work in the Soviet Union. Translation of *Not Without Laughter* into Russian had begun before he arrived and was completed while he waited to leave on the tour. In September, the Russian translation of his first two books of poetry got under way. And in Tashkent, the first stop on his tour, he would arrange for *The Weary Blues* to be translated into Uzbek. It was in the Soviet Union, then, that Hughes accomplished the goal that had so far eluded him in the United States, to make his living by his pen, while making the lives of black people his subject.

*Langston Hughes at age 14 (1916). Yale
Collection of American Literature, Beinecke
Rare Book and Manuscript Library.*

Langston Hughes and family (about 1916). L to R: Hughes, unidentified friend, Homer Clark, Gwyn "Kit" Clark, Carrie Clark. Yale Collection of American Literature, Beinecke Rare Book and Manuscript Library.

Hughes (center in white shirt and suspenders) in the USSR with film group and guides (1932). Yale Collection of American Literature, Beinecke Rare Book and Manuscript Library.

Hughes in Honolulu (1933). Yale Collection of American Literature, Beinecke Rare Book and Manuscript Library.

Chapter 12

SOVIET JOURNEY

Although he was among the most eager to tour Central Asia, Hughes decided to leave the group at Turkmenistan. He had secured a press permit that would allow him to remain in Central Asia after the tour group left, as well as a commission from the Soviet newspaper *Izvestia* to write a series of travel articles.

A five-day train journey brought the group of 11 Americans, an interpreter, a guide, and some trade union officials to Tashkent. They had particularly wanted to visit this district because of the parallels they saw between the condition of the peasants under the tsars and the condition of African Americans in the United States. Government officials were eager to show off their progress in expanding education and health care, modernizing agriculture, mitigating poverty, and improving the status of women. The group was restricted to organized tours and heard many long speeches, generally given in Russian, Uzbek, and English, in turn. The group then traveled to Samarkand and Bokhara, where they attended lectures and concerts and toured factories, farms, and hospitals.

Though impressed by the way dark-skinned minorities were treated, Hughes and the others began to grow weary of the tour and the endless rounds of speeches. The other members of the group voted to cut the tour short and return to Moscow, rather than spend two days in Ashkabad where Hughes had arranged to leave them. Hughes was angry, for he had counted on the assistance of the Soviet interpreter and guides in those days to help him get settled. Instead he got off the train alone.

The station was deserted and miles from the town, but the stationmaster was able to understand enough of Hughes's plight that he called the local newspaper editor who spoke French. This man gave Hughes a ride into town and found him a place to stay, but was unable to provide the interpreter Hughes needed in order to get to work on writing his articles for *Izvestia*.

Hughes spent a few days in the little town, befriending a Red Army captain from the Pamirs with whom he could communicate by signs only. This captain liked to listen to Hughes's jazz records and to take him to see the local circus perform. Just as Hughes was beginning to feel a little desperate about how, given the language barrier, he would learn enough about the local culture and conditions to write his articles, Arthur Koestler knocked on his door. Koestler (who would later write the anti-Communist novel *Darkness at Noon*) was a journalist from Berlin who was traveling through the USSR writing a series of articles. He spoke English and was then a Communist Party member, and through him Hughes was invited to meet government officials and heads of factories. He also became acquainted with Shaarieh Kikiloff, the head of the Turkoman Writers Union, and at last began to gather material for his articles. Kikiloff could translate Turkoman into Russian and Koestler could translate the Russian into English.

After about 10 days, Hughes, Koestler, Kikiloff, and a Ukranian named Kolya Shagurin obtained permission to travel as a "Writers Brigade," visiting various collective farms in the region. They traveled to Merv, and then Koestler and Hughes went alone to Permetyab and Bokahara. Everywhere Koestler was offended by the poverty and filth. Hughes agreed that Permetyab was horrible, yet even in this isolated desert refugee community where Soviet reforms had not yet penetrated he found something to praise. He interviewed a Russian nurse stationed there and later wrote an article extolling the Soviet government's efforts to improve health care for the refugees from Afghanistan and India. Furthermore, Hughes enjoyed himself in absorbing the local culture in Merv and Bokhara. In Merv, he visited a synagogue and interviewed Jews about the way Soviet reforms had improved their lives by outlawing discrimination. Yet he also realized that many Jews resented the party's attempts to suppress all forms of religious observance. Hughes noted that many other former synagogues in the city had been taken over and converted to warehouses or offices.

Upon Hughes's return to Tashkent he was able to collect a 6,000-ruble advance for his Uzbek book, which was the equivalent of more than he had ever been paid for any of his American publications. But he immediately fell ill. The first doctor he saw prescribed a medicine containing arsenic, which only made Hughes violently sick to his stomach. Fortunately, some visiting writers called on Hughes the next day and secured further medical attention.

After getting his strength back, Hughes began to wander the city interviewing people and taking notes for his articles. He particularly focused on the Uzbek regional theater and made it the subject of one of his *Izvestia* articles.

When he returned to Moscow in January, his travel permit had expired, and he could not find a hotel willing to rent him a room. He spent the first night in the lobby of the Hotel Savoy, and then went to call on Walt Carmon, editor of *International Literature*. Grateful for the chance to interview Hughes about his travel in Central Asia, Carmon invited Langston to stay with him until the Soviet government could provide a place for him. Hughes stayed a month in the four-room apartment that also housed Carmon's wife and two other American couples. One of the men was Jack Chen, of African and Chinese ancestries, whose sisters Yolande and Sylvia were also in Moscow and had visited Hughes when he had first arrived with the film group. Sylvia (who was also called Si-lan) was a dancer, and Hughes soon got to know her better. She was living at the Metropole Hotel, and Hughes frequently called on her after he secured a room at the new Moscow Hotel. A romance developed but was cut short by Chen's departure for a dance tour in the Crimea.

The couple exchanged wistful letters during her tour. As with Anne Cousey in Paris years before, Hughes seemed to have held back from any declaration of his feelings when Chen was available but was later inclined to make retrospective professions of love. Rampersad believes that despite the strong attraction Hughes felt, Hughes held back from pursuing Chen because the responsibilities of marriage would hinder his freedom as a poet (*LLH* I: 268). Faith Berry speculates that Hughes shied away from emotional commitments to women because of the emotional and financial demands his mother had placed on him after his father had left her (186). She also plausibly suggests that Hughes was battling his own homosexual inclinations and thus was unable to form a lifelong, intimate relationship with a woman (185). Rampersad, by contrast, questions the prevalent assumption that Hughes was homosexual and suggests that Hughes may have been "asexual" (*LLH* I: 289).[1] Publicly Hughes always presented himself as a heterosexual; but whatever his sexual orientation, his characteristic response to those who displayed or returned erotic interest was evasion. While Hughes had sexual encounters with both men and women, he seems never to have given himself wholly to any love affair. His history of conflict, manipulation, and abandonment with his parents and, later, with his patron appears to have created in him a resolve to hold himself aloof. Not allowing himself to form a passionate bond protected him from emotional vulnerability and guaranteed his creative independence.

Perhaps Hughes's involvement that spring with another woman, whom he called "Natasha" in his autobiography, was an attempt to exorcise the ghost of Sylvia with a relationship in which he had no emotional investment. While Sylvia is mentioned only in a single brief passage as "the girl [Hughes] was in love with that winter" (*IW* 256), Natasha's aggressive pursuit of Hughes dominates four chapters of *I Wonder as I Wander*. Natasha was an actress whom Hughes had met when attending a rehearsal at the Meyerhold Theater. After walking her home from the theater a few times and being introduced to her husband, Hughes escorted Natasha to a party where they stayed past the departure of the last streetcar. They were provided with cots in their hosts' kitchen, but the extreme cold prompted them to share a bed. Since Natasha was married, Hughes did not fear any serious entanglement even when a few nights later he found her waiting for him in his hotel room. Her friendship was useful to him for she knew her way around the bureaucracy and helped him arrange to return to the United States by way of China rather than through Europe as the film company had intended. But he found her frequent unannounced visits to his room annoying, particularly as they interfered with his writing.

Finally, his travel arrangements were successfully concluded despite a last-minute change, which forced Hughes to give up his plan of taking the train all the way to China. The Japanese, who had previously invaded Manchuria, now bombed Shanghai and refused to let the Soviet trains travel farther than Vladivostok. From there, Hughes would go by boat to Korea and Japan and then on to Shanghai.

A few days before his departure, Natasha came to Hughes's room claiming that she wanted to divorce her husband and marry Hughes. When he made clear that nothing of the sort was in his mind, she cried and protested loudly. To Hughes it seemed as if she were acting a part and he was relieved when she finally exhausted herself and left in a huff. But when Hughes boarded the train for Vladivostok, he was dismayed to discover that Natasha had booked passage on the same train. Once she realized that he was not eager to have her company on the 10-day journey, she wept again, but got off the train and returned to Moscow, leaving Hughes feeling guilty and relieved.

The 10-day ride on the world's longest railroad gave Hughes plenty of time to reflect on his Soviet adventure. The previous six months in Moscow had been a productive time for Hughes as a writer. Initially he had focused on journalism, writing for *Izvestia*, and *International Literature*. His essays were written in English and appeared in both English and a Russian translation. The essays for *Izvestia* were eventually collected in book form and published in Moscow as *A Negro Looks at Soviet Central Asia*. He also continued to write poetry. "Letter to the Academy" appeared in *International Literature* while "Ballad of the Landlord" appeared in *Krasnaya Nov* (CP 169, 402–3). In Moscow, he was able to support himself easily by what he made from his writing.

Toward the end of his stay, he began writing short stories for the first time since his college days. The inspiration came in part from his first reading of a collection by D. H. Lawrence, *The Lovely Lady*. Hughes aspired to write stories as "psychologically powerful" as Lawrence's and began a series of stories that dealt with the relationship between blacks and whites in America and would eventually be collected as *The Ways of White Folks*. Although the stories are not autobiographical, many of them comment indirectly on his failed relationship with his patron. Hughes observed that the title character of Lawrence's book reminded him of Godmother (*IW* 213). He sent Blanche Knopf three of the short stories he had written, and she sold two of them to the magazine *American Mercury*, recommending that in the future he hire Maxim Lieber as his agent for his magazine work. Hughes took her suggestion and Lieber continued to place the stories as he wrote them.

Other dealings with Knopf were less happy. His two children's books had been published in the fall of 1932 and both were widely praised, but *Popo and Fifina* had been published by Macmillan, not Knopf. Hughes failed to interest Blanche Knopf in publishing a manuscript based on his travel pieces, which he called "Dark People of the Soviet" (Bernard 102). Nor was Knopf impressed by a collection of his radical poems entitled *Good Morning, Revolution*, which Carl Van Vechten had also criticized. Individual poems, however, were published in *Opportunity*, the *Crisis*, and the *New Masses*.

Though Hughes had been looking forward to his visit to the Pacific, he found the Japanese military presence oppressive and was himself watched by the authorities as a possible subversive nearly everywhere he went. His Kyoto-bound boat stopped for a day at Seishin in Korea. Hughes and an Australian man took a walking tour with a little Korean boy as a guide and were trailed by two Japanese men who stayed a few yards behind them and never spoke to or acknowledged them, even when Hughes mockingly waved goodbye as he returned to the boat (*IW* 237–38).

After a night in Kyoto, Hughes took a train to Tokyo where he remained for two weeks. He made a point of visiting the progressive Tsukiji Theater. In Moscow he had met Seki Sano, its former director, who had written to his colleagues to expect Hughes's coming. They welcomed him warmly and in the days that followed took charge of showing him Japan.

He also gave several interviews and was invited to give a speech at the Pan-Pacific Club luncheon. Hughes's speech followed that of a white woman from St. Louis, the wife of an American official, who gave what Hughes deemed a condescending talk about the beauty of the Japanese tea ceremony. According to Hughes's account in *I Wonder as I Wander*, when he rose to speak he pointed out that in America, in the woman's hometown, he would not be able to eat lunch or even drink tea in a public place with her. He praised Japan for being a nation of dark people that had its own sovereign government and was free of the color line that western imperial powers had imposed on other Asian nations. However, in a reference to the government's aggression against China, he said that he hoped that the Japanese would never try to colonize others (242–43). Hughes claimed that his speech was received favorably by the audience though the American woman was offended. However, some were upset enough to distort his words. Nine years later, someone told the FBI that in this speech Hughes predicted a race war in which the dark peoples of the world would unite to subjugate the whites (qtd. in *LLH* I: 273).

Hughes then sailed for Shanghai where he stayed for three weeks. In the nineteenth century, a part of Shanghai was divided from the rest as the International Settlement and it was further subdivided into American, British, and French concessions, among others. Barbed wire and police patrols separated the international sections from the Chinese parts of the city, but Hughes explored both and claimed he felt more comfortable among the Chinese than among the Europeans who imposed a color line. His impressions of Shanghai were not favorable. He was appalled by the drug trade, prostitution of both children and adults, beggars who deliberately deformed themselves and their children to win more alms, and child factory labor. The Japanese had recently bombed one of the Chinese sections and there were Japanese patrols everywhere, along with dire predictions that they would soon take over the city.

Hughes requested an interview with Madame Sun Yat Sen, the sister-in-law of the Nationalist leader Chiang Kai-Shek and the widow of the founder of the Chinese Republic, and was instead invited to dine with her. He also visited Sun Yat Sen's grave in Nanking and met with Lu Hsun, a dissident poet. A group of progressive writers and journalists gave him a farewell party before he left China. These activities aroused the concern of the Japanese police who interrogated him upon his return to Tokyo. They questioned him closely about his activities and political beliefs for six hours, and then returned with him to his hotel room where they searched his belongings. Finally, they ordered him to leave Japan within two days and not to speak to any more Japanese people. Before leaving Japan, Hughes gave an interview to a *New York Times* reporter, and both the *Times* and the *Japan Times and Mail* reported his deportation. Another paper, the *Tokoyo Nichi Nichi*, offered a bogus "interview" with him in which he expressed support for Japanese imperialism, which in reality, he strongly condemned.

When Hughes's ship reached Honolulu, he was met by local newspapermen as well as an FBI agent. The agent did not question him, however, but merely listened as he gave an indignant account of his questioning in Japan to the reporters. Unknown to Hughes, an English translation of the notes the Japanese police made in their interview with him was eventually sent to the State Department and retained until after his death as part of a classified file on "The Communistic Activities of Langston Hughes" (Berry 195). In this document Hughes is quoted as claiming sympathy for the Communist Party's aims and its struggle on behalf of the "oppressed masses" while disavowing membership or any belief that Communism can bring about "complete freedom" (qtd. in Berry 197).

After talking with the reporters, Hughes enjoyed a day of sightseeing in Honolulu. At sunset his ship departed for San Francisco, where he sailed under the Golden Gate on August 9, 1933.

Note

1. Rampersad discusses this issue at length in his afterword to the second edition of the second volume of his biography of Hughes, published in February 2002.

Chapter 13

UNEASY IN CARMEL

Back in California, Hughes was once again the guest of Noël Sullivan. After a week at Sullivan's home, he moved into his guest cottage in Carmel. Hughes was offered the use of the cottage, rent-free for a full year. Sullivan also paid the utility bills and provided the groceries and a cook. Thus, Hughes once again found himself in the ironic position of being committed to socialism while being sheltered from the ravages of the depression that surrounded him by a wealthy white patron. Still, the situation was much different in that Sullivan, unlike Mason, did not try to exert any control over his writing and, at this point in their relationship, sympathized with Hughes's radical politics.

California had been particularly hard hit by the depression and had been the scene of much labor unrest the year before. Carmel remained a wealthy community but was suffering from declines in tourism. While most of the community was politically conservative, there was a small but active group of local radicals including the writers Orrick Jones and Lincoln Steffens. Ella Winter, the former wife of Steffens, had founded a chapter of the John Reed Club, an organization committed to leftist principles, which had about 30 chapters nationwide. Hughes had given a reading at a club meeting the year before, and now he began attending its Sunday night meetings, addressing the club again in October. The group gave their support to striking fishermen, cannery workers, and cotton workers, and Hughes joined them.

He also turned again to the Scottsboro cause, for the nine boys who had been convicted of raping two white women on a train in 1931 had been granted new trials. Hughes spoke at a rally in December and raised money for the accused boys' defense by arranging an auction of books, manuscripts, and artworks donated by distinguished authors and artists. The auction raised $1,400, 40 percent more than Hughes had expected (*LLH* I: 284).

Nevertheless, his main focus that fall was not activism, but writing. Hughes continued to write short stories and relied on Maxim Lieber, his new agent, to place them. Leiber sold "Slave on the Block," the third story Hughes had sent to Knopf from the Soviet Union, to *Scribner's* magazine, where it appeared in September. More difficult to place was "Home," a story about a lynching that was rejected by five magazines before eventually being accepted by *Esquire*. One editor criticized the story as one that strove "to lay the flesh bare and rub salt in the wound" rather than providing any pleasure for the reader (qtd. in *LLH* I: 282). *Esquire* also published "A Good Job Gone" in April 1934, after first publishing a plot synopsis, then inviting readers to vote on whether the story should be published. Their publicity campaign played up the story as breaking the taboo on writing about miscegenation, but what makes the story powerful is its frank portrayal of the point of view of its black characters. Pauline, the mistress of a wealthy white man who becomes obsessed with her, explains to the narrator that when one depends on white people for a living it is necessary to "make 'em think you like it." Although "just because they pay you they always think they own you," Pauline will not be controlled by her employer, nor will she hide her view of their liaison as strictly an economic relationship. She refuses to give up her black boyfriend even though it spells the end of her lucrative relationship with Mr. Lloyd, who then succumbs to alcoholism and insanity.

By December, Hughes had completed 12 stories, which he sent as a collection to both Van Vechten and Blanche Knopf for comment. This time the response was strong and positive, and Knopf accepted the manuscript for publication. Cheered by this success, Hughes decided to hire a secretary in order to write more productively. Roy Blackburn, a 22-year-old business-school graduate, accepted his offer of room, board, and 20 percent of the profits on all stories, poems, and articles to be written over the next six months.

Aside from continuing to work on short stories and magazine pieces, Hughes had three major projects in mind for 1934: revising "Good Morning, Revolution," the poetry collection that both Van Vechten and Knopf had disliked, making a second attempt at a manuscript about his Soviet travels, this time to be called "From Harlem to Samarkand," and writing a play in collaboration with Ella Winter that would tell the story of the recent cotton strike in San Joaquin Valley. He also continued to work on short stories, adding the story "Rejuvenation through Joy" to the collection Knopf was preparing for publication. Hughes sent Lieber five pieces based on his Soviet travels and Lieber surprised him by placing one, an interview with one of the former wives of the emir of Bokhara, in *Woman's Home Companion* for a payment of $400. Another story, "Why, You Reckon?" appeared in the *New Yorker* in March. He was also writing a few radical poems, including one for a Scottsboro rally entitled "One More S in the USA." The poem looks forward to a time when the United States would be sovietized; the land would belong to those who farmed it, and the factories to those who operated the machinery (CP 176).

As one of the most prominent black writers with radical leanings, Hughes was sought out by the Communist Party to be the president of the League of Struggle for Negro Rights, and he consented. The position was a nominal one; Hughes was merely lending his name to the cause rather than taking on an active role in the affairs of the organization. In April 1934, he was praised by Walt Carmon in the pages of the *New Masses* as one of the writers who was actively using his writing to further the cause of justice (Berry 209).

The Ways of White Folks, published that May, was a critical triumph for Hughes. Reviewers recognized the unity of the collection and its uniqueness in presenting, in Locke's words, "stories of Negro-white contacts told from the unusual angle of the Negro point of view" (66). In several of the stories, Hughes shows exactly what black Americans think of the whites who exploit them and expect them to be grateful for the exploitation. Hard-working servants like Cora of "Cora Unashamed" or the title character in "Berry" know they are being taken advantage of but keep working faithfully, not out of love for their employers nor because they are too ignorant to know better, but because "the teeth in the trap of economic circumstances" won't let them escape (4). In "A Good Job Gone," "Slave on the Block," "Poor Little Black Fellow," and "The Blues I'm Playing," the characters reject the benefits offered to them by wealthy whites because the price is too high in terms of human dignity. The whites are blind to their own faults and prejudices and are bewildered by the apparent ingratitude of those they sought to help. Two stories expose the horrors of lynching, and others, like "Passing," "Poor Little Black Fellow," and "One Christmas Eve," depict the psychological effects of racism. Some of the stories skewer the shallowness of some whites' embrace of black culture, particularly "Rejuvenation through Joy," in which whites are duped by a con-man who invites them to heal themselves through an embrace of the "primitive" music and dance of the Africans. Finally, many of the stories concern miscegenation, forcing readers to recognize the hypocrisy of a white America that fails to recognize its intimate relationship with its darker sisters and brothers.

The angry and ironic tone of the collection as a whole made some readers flinch. Probably recognizing that many of the stories could be subtle commentaries on the collapse of Hughes's patronage relationship with Godmother, Locke commented that had the book been written with "less resentment" it would have been a greater book (67). Sherwood Anderson felt that Hughes was unfair to whites. While the black characters were "alive, warm and real," the white characters "are all caricatures" (65). Some backlash was probably inevitable. Hughes had broken new ground, as Rampersad points out, by "risk[ing] the barbed wire and the minefields where two hostile races clash" (*LLH* I: 290). On the whole, the book was a dazzling achievement in the field of the short story, reaching heights that Hughes was never to attain again in fiction.

Perhaps feeling lonely as one of the only African Americans in Carmel, and also ready to romanticize a past relationship once the woman was comfortably out of reach, in January Hughes sent Sylvia Chen a letter inviting her to visit him. She replied that she was surprised to hear from him and had been hurt when he had stopped writing to her for such a long time. Hughes waited three months to reply, then sent her a telegram telling her he loved her and wanted her to come to him at once. Noticing that the telegram was dated April 1, Chen treated it lightly, but replied that she was glad to hear from him and might indeed come to visit him sometime soon. Again Hughes hesitated to reply and then in July sent a letter telling her how much he loved and missed her. In later letters he joked about having a baby with her, but he continued the pattern of writing an ardent letter followed by months of silence.

Chen was frustrated by Hughes's inconsistency and got tired of waiting for him to make a serious move. At roughly the same time Hughes sent her his first letter from Carmel, she met Jay Leyda, an American living in Moscow. He courted her, and she finally married him at the end of the summer of 1934. However, Chen did not tell Hughes of her marriage until 1936, despite occasionally corresponding with him. According to Chen, when she finally revealed her marriage, Hughes responded with an angry letter, which she destroyed. However, he later welcomed both her and her husband when they visited the United States in 1937 (qtd. in *LLH* I: 288). Faith Berry reports, presumably with reference to an interview with Chen, that sometime in 1937, Hughes met Sylvia in New York, brought her to meet a friend for tea, and then escorted her to the subway where he tearfully asked her how she could have given up their romance and married someone else (277). It is probable that if Chen had called his bluff and come to the United States, Hughes would have backed away, but in the spring and fall of 1934, marriage to Sylvia was still an enjoyable fantasy for Hughes to contemplate.

In the spring of 1934, Hughes completed the manuscript of "From Harlem to Samarkand" and sent it to Blanche Knopf, who soon rejected it. In April, he and Ella Winter began meeting several times a week to work on the play *Blood on the Fields*, a drama that told the story of a strike in San Joaquin Valley, which had taken place the previous fall. The fictional heroine of the play was based on Caroline Decker, who led the strike. In May, while they were still working on the play, the International Longshoreman's Association went on strike in California. While the John Reed Club supported the strike, most in Carmel were concerned with its negative impact on the economy and the papers were full of allegations that the strike was the fault of communist agitation. The rumors became more personal when the media alleged that Ella Winter was receiving money from the Soviet Union and funneling it to the strikers. Violence erupted when strikebreakers were brought in, and two strikers died. At a public meeting at which Hughes and Sullivan were present, residents of Carmel attacked the John Reed Club, and Hughes, visible as the groups' one black member, felt singled out for special hostility. Receiving threats, Hughes retreated to San Francisco rather than risk a visit from any Carmel vigilantes.

In San Francisco, Hughes finished *Blood on the Fields* but in a reversal of his experience with Zora Neale Hurston, Ella Winter asked him to take her name off the script before he tried to sell or produce it. She was worried about the reaction in Carmel, but Hughes insisted on acknowledging her as co-author when he copyrighted the play. The strike ended and Hughes felt safe enough to return to Carmel in August, but found himself ridiculed in the local newspaper by the editor E. F. Bunch who criticized him for spreading communism and appearing publicly with white women, and mocked those in the community who had actually treated him as a "distinguished guest." Hughes, Bunch contended, belonged in Russia, not Carmel (qtd. in *LLH* I: 294).

Hughes took the hint and left town again, the more willing perhaps because his year under Sullivan's patronage had ended. He decided to move on to Reno, Nevada, where he hoped to live cheaply and write steadily. He secured a room in a boarding house, returned to California for a month, and then took up residence in Reno in October. During his time in California he had written "On the Road," which was published in *Esquire,* as well as an account of his brush with the vigilantes in Carmel, which was sent to the *New Masses* but apparently not published there.

Meanwhile *Blood on the Fields* was rejected by the Theater Union, leading Winter and Hughes to bring in a third collaborator, Ann Hawkins, to revise the script. The new script was retitled *Harvest* but was never submitted to the Theater Union, as it had disbanded. The play remained unpublished until it was included in Susan Duffy's book, *The Political Plays of Langston Hughes*, in 2000.

Back in Reno, Hughes tried without much enthusiasm to work on his Soviet manuscript, but his confidence had been undermined by Knopf's rejection. His mother was pressuring him for money, explaining that it would be unacceptable for her to go on relief while she had a son who was a famous writer. But Langston himself was struggling. Despite its positive reviews, *The Ways of White Folks* was not selling well. He applied for a Guggenheim Fellowship to support work on a sequel to *Not Without Laughter*, but he also hit on another idea he thought would raise money. Why not use a pen name and write sentimental love stories featuring white characters? Maybe these would sell more readily to magazines, perhaps even to the movies. Hughes's first story in this vein was "Mail Box for the Dead," which was never published. He wrote four more and sent them to Lieber, asking him to place them under the name "David Boatman."

Meanwhile, in his own mailbox on November 5, Hughes found a letter from Mexico dated October 22. The Patiño sisters, friends of his father, had written to tell him that James Hughes was on his deathbed. Time and distance had softened some of Langston's anger toward his father, and he resolved to try and see him one last time. A second letter arrived the next day informing him that his father had undergone an operation on October 22 and had died, apparently just after the first letter was sent. Although Langston would be too late to see his father, the Patiño sisters urged him to come and wind up his father's business matters. By the time he arranged for a visa he had successfully borrowed a total of $300 for the trip from his publisher, Sullivan, and his father's brother, John Hughes, and had also received a check from *Esquire* for "On the Road."

Upon arrival in Mexico City in early December, Hughes stayed with the Patiño sisters. He discovered that his father had already had to sell most of his property, including the ranch, in order to pay medical bills stemming from treatment of his stroke in 1922 and its lingering aftereffects. The estate that remained was small and had been left to the Patiño sisters, since James had separated from his second wife. There was no mention of Langston in the will.

Hughes did not want to contest the will, but the Patiño sisters invited him to stay on with them while the will was probated and offered him an equal share of their inheritance. Though Hughes refused their offer at first, he eventually agreed to accept 25 percent of his father's bank accounts. He needed the money, for he had to pay back the loans he had received. Soon he heard from Lieber that the "white stories" he had written with the expectation that they were sure to be quickly published were being rejected. This was especially discouraging because Lieber had convinced him that three of the stories were so good they should be sent out under his own name after all. To have these stories rejected after Lieber's praise suggested to Hughes that white editors has rejected his work because of his race. The real problem, however, was not his lack of success as an author of "white stories" but his struggle to support himself financially as an acclaimed author of "black stories."

Hughes had spent the first several weeks in Mexico in obscurity, but, growing bored, he contacted José Antonio Fernández de Castro, his old friend from Cuba who was now with the Cuban embassy in Mexico City. He began to socialize with writers and artists and soon began translating the work of several writers. He collected these pieces in an anthology called "Troubled Lands," but Lieber was unenthusiastic after reading the manuscript. Eventually a few of the individual stories were placed in American magazines. Hughes moved out of the Patiño sisters' house into an apartment, which he shared with the young French photographer Henri Cartier-Bresson and a Mexican poet, Andres Henestrossa.

As summer approached, Hughes made plans to return to the United States for professional, personal, and political reasons. Certain writing projects called him back. He was awarded a $1,500 Guggenheim Fellowship to be paid over nine months to support his work on his proposed new novel. It was to be set in Chicago, so Hughes planned to move there for research after a brief stay in Los Angeles to work with Arna Bontemps on some children's stories. He also gave his consent for a weeklong production of *Mulatto* in Dobbs Ferry, New York, at the summer theater of Martin Jones. A successful production could lead to Broadway. On a personal level, his mother pleaded with him to come to her. She was lonely, still struggling financially, and worried that a lump in her breast might be cancerous.

But Hughes also returned for political reasons. In Mexico, he was cut off from the activities of the newly formed League of American Writers, affiliated with the International Union of Revolutionary Writers. Hughes had signed the open letter published in the *New Masses* that had called for the formation of such a group, but had not been present at the first American Writers' Congress in April. He had written a statement that was read at the Congress: "To Negro Writers." In this militant address Hughes called on black writers to expose several aspects of American life that hindered the progress of race relations and human rights for blacks, including suspect philanthropists who support black schools, but firmly believe in segregation, white union leaders who preach brotherhood but practice segregation, and black political or religious leaders who compromise their principles to appease the white establishment. Black writers could educate whites by creating black characters who were fully human and could awaken their black readers to radical ideas. These were strong words, which shed light on the mood behind *The Ways of White Folks*, much as "The Negro Artist and the Racial Mountain" had illuminated his first books of poetry and *Not Without Laughter*. Unfortunately, Hughes found it hard to live up to the goals he himself set. His own writing had begun to founder and would continue to do so over the next few years.

Chapter 14

ADRIFT

Hughes spent three months in California upon his return from Mexico. Though he did visit Sullivan briefly in Carmel, he stayed primarily in Los Angeles. He and Arna Bontemps worked on a children's story set in Mexico that aimed to repeat the success of *Popo and Fifina*, but this time they expected to be able to command a substantial advance. Unfortunately, Macmillan rejected their manuscript, "The Paste-Board Bandit," as well as a second collaboration, "Bon-Bon Buddy." Lieber urged Hughes to stop wasting time on juvenile stories and to return to more mature themes (*LLH* I: 308). Meanwhile Hughes tried unsuccessfully to be hired as a Hollywood writer and asked Lieber to try to arrange some lectures for him.

Hughes was supposed to speak at a YMCA in Los Angeles as part of a memorial service sponsored by the Los Angeles Civic League, but the YMCA cancelled the program because Hughes was allegedly "anti-Christian" and a Communist. This action was unexpected and disturbing to Hughes. He wrote and sold a few short stories, but otherwise his California stay was disappointing. On a brighter note, however, he met the actor Clarence Muse and the black composer William Grant Still, with whom he discussed collaborating on his long-neglected project of an opera about Haiti. In September, he traveled to Oberlin, Ohio, to join his mother.

Hughes remained in Ohio only a few weeks before moving on to New York. John R. Rumsey was acting as Hughes's drama agent and had arranged for the Dobbs Ferry production of *Mulatto*. Audience reaction had been positive, and now Martin Jones sought an option on the play with a right to hire a playwright to improve the final act. Hughes consented and agreed that the new playwright would receive 25 percent of the royalties. Hughes was surprised to find the play already in rehearsal when he arrived in New York on September 27 although, contrary to the impression Hughes gave in *I Wonder as I Wander,* he did, indeed, know that a production was planned for sometime that fall and had consented to let another playwright make changes to the script. What Hughes discovered now was that it was Jones himself who was rewriting the end of the play. Hughes wasn't happy with his changes, which sensationalized the play, adding more sex and violence, including the rape of the sister of the hero. Despite his misgivings, the tantalizing prospect of a Broadway production made him willing to go along.

As the opening night approached, Jones demanded a royalty increase to 35 percent and billing as a co-author of the play. Hughes gave in to these demands but insisted on collecting the full $500 advance he was promised, despite Jones's arguments that it be proportionately reduced along with the royalties. Jones further angered Hughes by not inviting any blacks involved in the production to the post-production party. When Hughes learned this, he refused to attend the premiere.

Reviewers praised the acting but harshly attacked the script. The response was partly a reaction to the play's explosive subject matter, but Hughes felt that the critical rejection of the play was mainly the result of Jones's tampering, which had distorted the script. To escape the depressing reviews, Hughes hastily left New York and, on the train to Oberlin, wrote the poem "Let America Be America Again." The poem contrasts the ideal of America as a place of freedom, equality, and opportunity with the realities facing the immigrant, the red man, the poor white, and the Negro. The speaker points out that "America never was America to me," yet does not give up hope that America can live up to its promise (*CP* 189–91). This was the second great poem that Hughes composed on a train, the first being "The Negro Speaks of Rivers" in 1919. The poem was published by *Esquire* in 1936 but the magazine, with Hughes's reluctant permission, cut the final third of the poem, where Hughes calls for the disenfranchised to "take back our land" from "those who live like leeches on the people's lives." The poem became a public favorite, prominently featured by Hughes in many of his poetry readings.

Hughes was concerned with his mother's health. Carrie had at last consented to have an examination and cancer had been confirmed, but now she resisted having surgery. An offer from Rowena Jelliffe in Cleveland gave Hughes the opportunity to remain somewhat close to his mother while furthering his work as a dramatist. The Gilpin Players were seeking a resident playwright to write suitable plays for a black cast. Hughes accepted the offer and began working on a comedy. The play, *Little Ham,* focused on participants in the "numbers racket" in Harlem, and the Gilpin Players paid him $50 to do five performances. In January, he found Carrie a room in Cleveland that was close to a clinic where she could go for electrotherapy treatment.

Despite the negative reviews of *Mulatto*, to Hughes's great surprise the production was still running at year's end. Hughes had not received his share of the royalties. In fact, Jones had not even sent any financial statements, which were supposed to be due weekly. Jones claimed that the play was losing money, but in any case royalties were due on box-office receipts, not profits. As in the *Mule Bone* case, Hughes asked Arthur Spingarn to help him secure his rights, but he was angry and frustrated. Just before Christmas, Jones finally sent Hughes a statement, which showed that Hughes was due $88.50 in royalties. No check was enclosed. Instead, pleading that the show was not yet profitable, Jones asked him to waive royalties for the present, or the show would be closed. Hughes refused to give in and, in January, Jones paid him $88, but then demanded that his own share of future royalties be increased another 10 percent. The dispute was referred to the Dramatists Guild for arbitration and a few months later, Hughes prevailed.

Hughes had taken a brief trip to Chicago in December with the money from *Little Ham*. He needed to begin his research for his novel. Bontemps had moved there from California, and during Hughes's visit, the two writers finished a draft of a folk play called *When the Jack Hollers*. Hughes had decided to use his Guggenheim money to travel to Spain and write his novel there. Therefore he had postponed the start of the grant until March 1936 and was unable to draw on those funds when he returned to Chicago in January to continue his research and work on revising the play with Bontemps. Hughes hated the cold and the harsh conditions on Chicago's South Side and continued to struggle financially.

In the past, lectures had been a reliable source of income, but now Hughes found that many organizations rejected him as too radical. He did give a prominent address on January 3 at the Third U.S. Congress against War and Fascism, but this did nothing to quash that view of him. His work, however, inconsistently represented his principles. Lieber questioned his decision to write comedies like *Little Ham* and *When the Jack Hollers* rather than serious works that grappled with important social issues, but when Hughes did write a radical play called *Angelo Herndon Jones*, the Gilpin Players turned it down, though the script went on to win a contest sponsored by the magazine *New Theater*.

In March, *Little Ham* was successfully produced by the Gilpin Players at Karamu House, but Hughes, sick with influenza, was unable to attend the premiere. Because the play was a success with both the audience and the critics, Jelliffe agreed to do *When the Jack Hollers* as the next production at Karamu House. Although the Guggenheim Fellowship had now begun and would last through the end of the year, Hughes did not leave for Spain as anticipated. His mother had gone into the hospital and then begun to recover, and Hughes wanted to be close to her. He also wanted to be available for the next Karamu production. Furthermore, he found he had little interest in writing his novel. Instead, he turned to two older projects, writing a libretto for an opera about Haiti, and reworking *Blood on the Fields*, the unpublished play he had written with Ella Winter.

In April, Hughes finally received a little over $300 from Jones for *Mulatto*, but *When the Jack Hollers* was neither a critical nor a popular success. Hughes then decided to turn away from comedy and submitted a version of his play about Haiti to Karamu House as his next project. The Spanish Civil War began in July, making Hughes glad he had not gone to Spain. *Troubled Island*, a nonmusical version of the Haiti play, was produced in November, and the positive reaction encouraged Hughes to go ahead with his idea of making it into an opera, with William Grant Still providing the score.

At the premiere of the play *Troubled Island*, Hughes was introduced to Elsie Roxborough. A black debutante from Detroit who was passionately interested in theater and had written a play about a woman who passes for white, Roxborough was eager to meet Hughes and hoped that they might collaborate on various projects. She was instantly smitten with Langston and, after getting drunk at the post-production party, she astonished him with a marriage proposal that he politely refused. She soon apologized for getting carried away and a friendship developed. Hughes agreed to let her theater troupe, the Roxanne Players, produce his play in Detroit.

Although the evidence does not suggest that he was ever even as serious about Elsie as he was about Sylvia Chen, perhaps he was less eager to discourage Roxborough's affections because a few months earlier he had received the letter in which Chen confessed her marriage to Jay Leyda. Over the next few months, Roxborough continued to pursue Hughes aggressively, repeatedly proposing marriage, while he claimed that his finances made taking a wife out of the question. Suddenly in March 1937, several black newspapers carried the news that Hughes and Roxborough were engaged. When Hughes angrily accused Roxborough of starting the rumor, she denied it but asked him to let the story fade gradually rather than humiliate her by publicly refuting it. However, Hughes was quoted in the *Baltimore Afro-American*, denying that he had any intention of marrying anyone, though when asked if he were in love with Roxborough, he gallantly allowed, "That much certainly could be true" (qtd. in *LLH* I: 333). Having made his utter lack of matrimonial intentions clear, Hughes was willing to attend the premiere of the Roxanne Players' performance of his play, which was now called *Drums of Haiti*. Their alleged romance received no further public attention.

In *I Wonder as I Wander*, Hughes claims that he was in love with Roxborough in 1937 and that he wrote to her from Spain. In her reply she advised him of her intention to pass for white and Hughes comments that she had "disappeared into the white world" by the time he returned in 1938 (*IW* 329). In fact, though she eventually dyed her hair blonde and worked as a "white" model under the name "Pat Rico," she occasionally wrote to Hughes through the early 1940s. At the time she died of a drug overdose in 1949, she was still passing for white, living in New York as "Mona Manet." Sometime after her death, Hughes began displaying in his study a photograph of her that she had inscribed to him in 1937. As with Anne Cousey and Sylvia Chen, though Hughes was unwilling to be a husband, he readily represented himself as a man who had loved and lost.

The Guggenheim grant ended in December 1936 without Hughes making any progress toward his novel, nor had he published anything with Knopf in the past three years. His revolutionary poems, which had been twice rejected by Blanche Knopf, now, through the efforts of Louise Thompson, found a publisher in the International Workers Order. As it would be only a 31-page booklet, a selection of poems was chosen, and the title, *A New Song*, was taken from one of the poems. The booklet included the full text of "Let America Be America Again." Hughes finished selecting the poems in March, but it would be more than a year before the booklet, which sold for 15 cents, was actually published. Meanwhile Karamu House put on another of Hughes's plays, but *Joy to My Soul*, a comedy about life in a black hotel, was dismissed as insignificant by the critics, though the mostly black audiences found it funny. *Mulatto* royalties were now being paid regularly, and according to Rampersad, amounted to nearly $4,000 for 1936 (*LLH* I: 334). Unfortunately, his mother's medical and living expenses consumed a good portion of that money.

Toward the end of April, Hughes headed out to California to work with William Grant Still on the opera based on *Troubled Island*. He also paid a visit to Noël Sullivan, who had purchased a new property called Hollow Hills Farm. Sullivan was glad to have Hughes visit, but asked him to please not discuss "the Russian experiment" with him, because he had become disillusioned with communism (qtd. in *LLH* I: 337). Meanwhile Hughes, in several instances, had declined speaking engagements that would openly link him with the Communist Party. However, he refused to speak against them as well, even though the trials of Trotsky and his followers had angered many who had formerly admired communism. In fact, Hughes had just allowed his name to appear as one of more than one hundred progressive American authors who signed a statement defending the trials as legitimate "efforts of the Soviet Union to free itself from insidious internal dangers" and affirming the importance of the Soviet Union in the fight against fascism (*LLH* I: 374; Berry 287).[1]

As Rampersad points out, Hughes was well aware that the strongest opponents of communism were the same people who tried to block the social and political advancement of blacks (*LLH* I: 338). Hughes was not willing, then, to stand against the Communists. Hughes had declined the first invitation to speak at the Second International Writers Congress in June 1937, perhaps partly because he was cooling toward the left, but more likely because it interfered with a planned study tour of Europe and the Soviet Union that he had been hired to lead. When the escalating war in Spain cancelled the tour and delayed the conference (which was relocated to Paris), Hughes cabled the organizers that he would like to come after all. Before he left he also signed an agreement with three black newspapers to work as a foreign correspondent, though the State Department declined to issue him press credentials. He sailed for Europe on the last day of June, glad to have a direction after nearly three years of being adrift politically, personally, and most of all, professionally.

Note

1. A version of this statement was published at least twice—in *The Daily Worker* in August, 1938 (*LLH* I: 374) and in *International Literature* 7 (1938): 104 (Berry 354).

Chapter 15

UNDER FIRE

On his way to cover the Spanish Civil War for several black newspapers, Hughes went first to Paris, where he was reunited with Henri Cartier-Bresson, the photographer who was his roommate briefly in Mexico. Cartier-Bresson was an ardent admirer of jazz, and together the two men visited various Parisian nightclubs. Hughes also found time to be lionized by several young black writers from French colonies, who acknowledged Hughes as a great influence on the development of their writing and the concept of Négritude. These included Aimé Césaire of Martinique, Léon Damas of French Guinea, and Léopold Sédar Senghor of Senegal. Hughes also spent time with Nicolás Guillén and Jacques Roumain, poets he had known in Cuba and Haiti; both had become Communists and had spent time in prison for their beliefs.

At the Paris sessions of the Second International Writers Congress against Fascism, Hughes gave an important address in which he proclaimed that American Negroes understood and opposed fascism since they lived with it every day. Recent events in Ethiopia, Germany, China, Italy, and Spain only showed that the "economic and social discrimination" directed against blacks in America was now being applied to oppressed groups worldwide (qtd. in *LLH* I: 334). Responding to the Italian invasion of Ethiopia, Hughes had also made the connection between fascism and racism in the poems "White Man" (*CP* 194–95) and "Air Raid over Harlem" (*CP* 185–88). He would continue to make the connection in other poems such as "Letter from Spain" and "Postcard from Spain," both of which attempt to give the perspective of black American soldiers fighting in the International Brigades (*CP* 201, 202).

After the conference Hughes and Guillén moved on to Spain. Barcelona had just been bombed, and Hughes was conscious of moving into danger. On his third night in Barcelona he was caught in his first air raid, and he later vividly evoked this experience in the poem "Air Raid: Barcelona" (CP 207):

Black smoke of sound
Curls against the midnight sky.
Deeper than a whistle,
Louder than a cry,
Worse than a scream
Tangled in the wail
Of a nightmare dream,
The siren
Of the air raid sounds.

. . .

All other noises are deathly still
As blood spatters the wall
And the whirling sound
Of the iron star of death
Comes hurtling down.
No other noises can be heard
As a child's life goes up
In the night like a bird. (1–9, 39–46)

Unharmed, Hughes and Guillén traveled next to Valencia; they reached Madrid in mid-August, where they stayed at the local headquarters of the Alianza de Intelectuales Antifascistas (Alliance of Antifascist Intellectuals) where artists and writers gathered to create propaganda for the Loyalist cause. At the Alianza, Hughes met many writers, including Ernest Hemingway, Lillian Hellman, and Dorothy Parker. In the town of Quijorna, Hughes was sickened by the sight and smell of detached body parts left behind after sustained aerial bombing, and was shot at by snipers.

Hughes was particularly interested in race relations in Spain and the effect of Franco's having recently brought in Moors from Morocco to fight against the government. Hughes wondered how the dark men on either side, the Moors fighting for Franco or the American blacks who had volunteered for the International Brigades, were faring. He met an African fighting on the loyalist side who said he did so in hopes that a government victory would result in better treatment of Spain's colonies. In radio broadcasts from Spain, Hughes told of the brave black American volunteers who were fighting fascism because it preached white supremacy. He emphasized the lack of color prejudice in Spain and noted that in this struggle blacks sometimes commanded white troops.

Hughes's dispatches were sent to both the *Baltimore Afro-American* and to the Associated Negro Press for distribution to various outlets. He also published in the *Volunteer for Liberty*, a periodical put out by the Fifteenth International Brigade. One poem that appeared there was "Roar China" which celebrated the combined resistance of Communist Party and Kuomintang forces against Japan in northern China and included imagery drawn from his visit to Shanghai in 1933 (*CP* 198–200).

Hughes remained in Madrid until mid-November. He was always in some danger. Bombs wounded over 3,000 people and killed about 1,000 during the time he was there (*LLH* I: 354). Hughes himself was once mildly wounded by sniper fire. With his journalistic obligations fulfilled, winter coming on, and food growing ever more scarce, Hughes reluctantly decided it was time to leave. He spent a month in Paris, and then arrived home in January.

Back in New York, Hughes moved in with Toy and Emerson Harper, old friends of his family, and finding himself once again in financial straits, he gratefully accepted a series of lectures arranged for him by Louise Thompson under the auspices of the International Workers Order (IWO), the organization that would soon publish his booklet *A New Song*. Hughes also enlisted Thompson's help in a new project. In 1931, he had tried to set up a revolutionary group in New York called the Suitcase Theater. Now he appealed to Louise to persuade the IWO to help him set up a theater of his own to produce plays for the cause of antifascism and socialism. Within weeks, the Harlem Suitcase Theater was established as cultural activity of the IWO, which allowed it space on the second floor of the IWO Community Center. At Thompson's suggestion, Hughes's first project was a "poetry play," a one-act play that incorporated recitations of many of his poems. He immediately set to work on the script and named the play *Don't You Want to Be Free?*

As executive director of the theater, Hughes decided to do shows in a theater-in-the-round style with no curtain and only minimal props or sets. He was committed to making music and dance integral to the action. He originally planned for the first production to feature a dance performance showcasing the history of black dance to be followed by a performance of *Don't You Want to Be Free?* Hilary Phillips would direct the production since Hughes had to leave on the lecture tour Thompson had arranged. But first he rented an apartment at 66 St. Nicholas Place for one year.

When Hughes returned, he decided to cancel the dance performance because he felt the dancers did not meet his professional standards. Still, he pressed on with *Don't You Want to Be Free?* The booklet *A New Song*, containing some of the poems in the play, was published just before the first performance on April 21, which was well attended. The play began with a young man declaring that the play was about himself and then identifying himself by reciting Hughes's poem "The Negro." From there, the play moved through various Hughes poems, recited by actors and interspersed with interludes of blues and spirituals. The production was extremely well received in Harlem, though critical reaction was less enthusiastic among Marxist critics who perhaps recognized that the poem was more a racial drama than a Marxist one. The play was also performed as the inaugural production for newly launched black drama groups in several other cities and was published that October in the magazine *One Act Play*.

With the success of the theater group Hughes made plans to have his belongings moved from storage in Cleveland and New Jersey to his Harlem apartment. But his happiness was marred by the death of his mother on June 3, 1938. The cancer had spread to her lungs.

In July, Hughes was invited back to Paris for an international conference: The Congress for Peace Action and against Bombing of Open Cities. When Hughes returned to New York, he found that the Harlem Suitcase Theater had made scant progress in preparing for the new fall season. Hughes decided that the play he had in mind to write for the Gilpin Players might also do for the Suitcase group and quickly wrote another one-act play in the style of *Don't You Want to Be Free?* However, both theater groups disliked the resulting play, *Young Man of Harlem*. Hughes promised to write something else for the Gilpin Players, envisioning a three-act play to be called *Front Porch*. This would need to be ready in time for their mid-November opening. Meanwhile, with no play ready for the Harlem Suitcase Theater, Hughes decided to revive *Don't You Want to Be Free?* much to the dissatisfaction of many of the players. He also had difficulty meeting the expenses to keep the theater going. *Mulatto* was still touring but Hughes was again having trouble collecting his royalties.

Pushed for time as he tried simultaneously to work on *Front Porch*, prepare some satirical skits to be performed by the Harlem Suitcase Theater, supervise the rehearsals of those skits and *Don't You Want to be Free?*, and collaborate with composer James P. Johnson on *The Organizer*—a play he began writing in Paris—Hughes had sent the Gilpin Players only the first act of *Front Porch* by October 19. After November 2, Jelliffe, in desperation, finished the third act herself. Hughes also wrote a third act, but either it arrived too late, as Jelliffe maintains, or else, as Hughes indicated in a note on his script, Jelliffe rewrote it because the cast found his ending too bleak. The play satirizes a black bourgeois family, and in the version Hughes wrote, the daughter of the family, pregnant by a black labor organizer, is pressured into an abortion and then dies. Her lover's strike fails. In Jelliffe's upbeat final act, the daughter defies her parents' demand that she get an abortion and goes to live with her lover, whose strike is successful. The Gilpin Players performed the Jelliffe version to tepid reviews. Meanwhile the Suitcase Theater opened its season with a reprise of *Don't You Want to Be Free?* and Hughes and Johnson completed *The Organizer*, which went into rehearsal at the Suitcase Theater.

Subletting his apartment and leaving Thompson and Phillips once again in charge of the theater, Hughes met Bontemps in Chicago where they began a lecture tour that took them through the Southwest to Los Angeles. One of their engagements was in Denver, where several hotels refused to lodge them. Reaching Los Angeles in December, the two began visiting schools and giving talks on "How Stories and Poems Are Born" and "Making Words Sing, Talk and Dance." Their lectures were sponsored by the Philippa Pollia Foundation, which continued to fund some appearances by Hughes alone after Bontemps returned to Chicago.

The lectures were not enough to keep him in Los Angeles. The real reason Hughes remained there instead of returning to the Harlem Suitcase Theater was to work with Clarence Muse. Muse was then running a Federal Theatre Project for which he had successfully staged Hall Johnson's play, *Run, Little Children*. Through Muse's efforts, Hughes received a contract from the Federal Theatre Project for $1,200 for three months' work revising the script of *St. Louis Woman*, an adaptation of Bontemps's novel *God Sends Sunday* that had been written by Countee Cullen and Bontemps. Everyone involved hoped that a Federal Theatre staging of Hughes's version of this play might lead either to a Broadway production or to a Hollywood film. Hughes strove to keep all parties happy and keep contract negotiations going smoothly.

Meanwhile Muse and Hughes were involved in another project as well. Muse had been offered the chance to develop a movie for the white child actor and singer Bobby Breen and asked Hughes to help. The movie was to be set in the South and to include spirituals. Hughes and Muse were each paid $150 for their synopsis and then $125 a week while they worked on the script, which was eventually titled *Way Down South*. Hughes suffered some humiliations in his encounters with openly racist Hollywood executives and must have had to swallow some scruples in creating a script full of Uncle Tom-like, long-suffering, but devoted slaves. Hughes also founded a new drama group, the New Negro Theater, which performed *Don't You Want to Be Free?* in March. Meanwhile personality conflicts were causing difficulties for the Harlem Suitcase Theater, but Hughes was too busy in California to come back and put things in order.

In April, with the two Los Angeles scripts completed, Hughes and Bontemps reunited for a Midwestern tour that included stops in eight states. Spain had just fallen to Franco, and Hughes spoke passionately about fascism abroad and racism at home. Hughes then settled into a hotel room in Chicago and began to work on his autobiography, a project both Van Vechten and Blanche Knopf had long wanted him to write. When he began to run out of money at the end of May, he asked Sullivan if he could stay with him while he finished his book and was at once invited to Hollow Hills Farm.

Before returning to California, however, Hughes went to New York where he gave a powerful speech at the Third American Writers' Congress. The thrust of the speech was a comparison of the situation of Jews in Germany with that of blacks in America. Hughes opined that except for the freedom of speech that the United States provided there was little difference. Furthermore, important avenues for disseminating speech, such as magazines, newspapers, and filmmaking were often inaccessible to blacks. He protested that Hollywood was uninterested in making realistic and meaningful pictures about African Americans, but instead depicted them as merely "servants, clowns and fools" (qtd. in *LLH* I: 370). Perhaps he was thinking guiltily of his own work on *Way Down South*, which indeed included such stereotypes.

Resigning as director of the Harlem Suitcase Theater because he did not anticipate returning to New York in the near future, Hughes attended the premiere of *Way Down South* in Los Angeles. He received credit as scriptwriter and had also written the lyrics for two of the songs. The film got positive reviews in the white press but was criticized by blacks and some critics on the left as depicting blacks in a stereotypical and demeaning fashion. In an unpublished statement "To My Public," Hughes justified himself by comparing the money he had earned from *Way Down South* to that from *Don't You Want to Be Free?* He pleaded the need to write some commercially viable material in order to avoid starvation and be able to write more serious work ("Statement in Round Numbers").

The serious work he wanted to attend to in the late summer of 1939 was his autobiography, *The Big Sea*, but world events proved distracting. As in 1938, Hughes had consented to have his name included as a signatory to an open letter. This one urged support for the Soviet Union as an important ally in the fight against fascism. Signed by more than 400 writers and intellectuals, it also denied that Stalin's regime was a totalitarian one. It was published in the *Daily Worker* on August 14, 1939, just days before the revelation that the USSR and Nazi Germany had signed a nonaggression pact. Hughes had difficulty reconciling the Soviet Union's alliance with fascism with his own observation and belief that the USSR had achieved a utopia of racial equality. Many former supporters of the Soviet Union now expressed their bitterness and disillusionment, but Hughes made no public statements. Instead, he wrote to Thompson that he thought it best to abandon political writing in such a complex environment, concentrating instead on race (qtd. in *LLH* I: 375). In *The Big Sea*, finished in the fall of 1939 and published the following August, he was deliberately apolitical, ending his story in 1931, and thus leaving out his trip to the Soviet Union, his association with leftist organizations and publications, and all of his radical poetry.

Having decided to stop writing radical verse and all forms of drama, Hughes began writing blues poems again, including a group of related poems called "Seven Moments of Love: An Un-Sonnet Sequence in Blues," which was published in the May 1940 issue of *Esquire*. To Blanche Knopf he proposed a collection of lighter verse including ballads, dialect poems, and blues lyrics. About half were recently written poems and the rest older, uncollected pieces. She asked for some time to consider the manuscript, and also turned down his request to bring out a cheap edition of *Not Without Laughter* that he could sell on the tour he planned to take in the spring of 1940.

The tour lasted from February until May and Hughes found it exhausting and barely profitable. His average fee was only about $35 (*LLH* I: 382) and he had to travel by train. His spirits were low. Not only was there frightening news from Europe, but Hughes could not help contrasting his precarious financial position with that of Richard Wright, whose first novel, *Native Son*, had just been selected as the January 1940 Book-of-the-Month Club offering. The book offers a harsh and disturbing view of black life in Chicago and explores the economic and social forces that lead the protagonist, Bigger Thomas, to become a murderer. Hughes had met Wright in Chicago in 1936, and had considered dramatizing one of his stories for the Suitcase Theater. Wright had given a lecture on Hughes's work and the two had collaborated on a poem "Red Clay Blues," published in *New Masses* the previous August. Hughes wrote to congratulate Wright, but privately and in a public forum at the Chicago Public Library, he expressed reservations about the novel. It would have been difficult not to feel some envy, or to wonder whether he had erred in abandoning his own planned novel of Chicago's South Side.

In the summer of 1940, an American Negro Exposition was planned for Chicago with Bontemps as cultural director. Hughes was offered a job

writing the script for two shows, "Jubilee: A Cavalcade of the Negro Theatre," which would feature scenes from various musicals, and an original
review called "The Tropics After Dark." Unfortunately, mismanagement
and corruption plagued the exposition and crowds were small. The first
show was never mounted, the second used only in a scaled-down version
with Hughes's dialogue removed, and Hughes was not paid for work on either.

Pinning his hopes on the success of *The Big Sea*, Hughes eagerly involved himself in publicity efforts. Positive reviews appeared in both
Newsweek and the *New York Times*. In Los Angeles, where Hughes traveled in the fall in order to work on a "Negro Revue" for the Hollywood
Theatre Alliance, he tried to promote the book whenever possible. Unable to find lodging in Hollywood where blacks were not welcome as residents, he endured a long commute from the Clark Hotel to his job on the
Revue. Working as a lyricist, he hoped that one of the songs would catch
on and make him rich. His highest hopes were for a number called "America's Young Black Joe."

On November 15, Hughes was preparing to speak at a "Book and Author" luncheon at a prominent hotel when followers of evangelist Aimee
Semple McPherson arrived to picket the hotel. While a sound track
blared "God Bless America," the picketers handed out copies of "Goodbye
Christ" and urged would-be attendees to skip the luncheon rather than
listen to a reading by a Communist and anti-Christian author. When the
hotel appeared ready to cancel the event, Hughes decided to withdraw.
He was badly embarrassed and discouraged by the incident and left Los
Angeles within the month.

Back in Carmel, settling into a small cottage that Sullivan had had
built for him, Hughes was dismayed to find that he was still under fire.
The *Saturday Evening Post* reprinted McPherson's handbill in the December 21 issue. Soon afterward, Stanford University cancelled a planned lecture by Hughes. Desperate, Hughes wrote out a statement repudiating the
poem. He claimed that he had written the poem in a spirit of youthful rad-
icalism, and that even so he was only taking on a communist point of view
for dramatic purposes, not expressing his true feelings. The poem was an
attack on those who exploit religion, not on Christianity itself. Furthermore, he had already withdrawn the poem from circulation and had not
given permission for it to be reprinted. Hughes sent the statement to
Knopf and to the Associated Negro Press but was aware that some of his
friends and acquaintances disapproved of him for giving into public pressure and disowning the poem. He must have been dismayed by the con-
temptuous response in the *People's World*, which mocked him for

repudiating the poem and for writing jingoistic songs (in a reference to "America's Young Black Joe") (qtd. in *LLH* I: 394–95).

Around the time that this item was published, Hughes was being admitted to the hospital. His health had gradually collapsed. In December and January, he suffered from toothache, sinusitis, fever, and pains in his left leg. He wrote to friends that it might be a bad case of influenza, but he actually had contracted a venereal disease a few weeks earlier.[1] In the days before penicillin, gonorrhea was difficult to treat, and Hughes remained in the hospital for two weeks on a high dose of sulfa drugs that made him drowsy and suppressed his appetite.

Bad news poured in. Sales of *The Big Sea* were disappointing, and the tenants to whom he had sublet his Harlem apartment had failed to pay the rent, leading to his eviction. Toy Harper had to rescue his belongings. Hughes had long since left the bombs of Spain behind him but sick, broke, and criticized for both the sentiments in "Good-bye Christ" and for repudiating those sentiments, he felt as if he were still under fire.

Note

1. Rampersad discovered the real nature of Hughes's illness by reading the patient records from his hospital stay. Hughes never acknowledged that he had gonorrhea in any of his known correspondence. For example, after he was released from the hospital Hughes wrote to Arna Bontemps: "Acute arthritis is really something, had me groggy with pain and pills!" (Nichols 72). Judging from the stage of the infection at the time of his admission, he probably contracted the disease during his stay in Los Angeles, but there are no clues as to the identity of his partner (*LLH* I: 394).

Chapter 16

FIGHTING HITLER
AND JIM CROW

Hughes was released from the hospital on the first day of February and headed for Hollow Hills Farm to convalesce. He stayed in the main house for the first few weeks while he regained his strength, and Sullivan lent him the money to settle his medical bills. Hughes was very short on funds, which led to a humiliating exchange with his publisher. When Hughes applied for a $400 loan, a representative of Knopf declined to advance that sum, pointing out that in 1940 the royalties from all five of his books amounted to only $111.15. However, if Hughes wished to sell his books to Knopf outright, a payment of $400 would be extended in place of any future royalty payments. Reluctantly, Hughes agreed to the proposal (*LLH II*: 10).

This wasn't his only tension with Knopf. Rejecting all of Hughes's suggestions, Blanche Knopf had chosen a white illustrator, E. McKnight Kauffer, to illustrate his forthcoming book of poetry, *Shakespeare in Harlem*. Hughes found these illustrations stereotypical and feared some of his readers would take offense.

Remembering the reaction to his screenplay *Way Down South*, Hughes may also have had some qualms about how black audiences might react to a radio series he had agreed to write for Moe Gale, a producer and one of the founders and owners of the Savoy Ballroom, a famous Harlem dance hall and nightspot. The series would be an *Amos and Andy*-like comedy featuring the main character of Hughes's play *Little Ham*. The *Amos and Andy* radio series was written and acted by whites and was highly popular with white audiences, but many blacks felt it was demeaning. Hughes himself had been criticized in the past for writing about the seamier side of Harlem life, and Hamlet Hitchcock Jones, the main character of the proposed series, was a numbers runner. Nevertheless Hughes quickly wrote two sample episodes that met with Gale's approval. If a sponsor could be found, Hughes would earn between $75 and $400 for each of the 16 episodes. Gale was unable to secure a sponsor, however, and Hughes's dreams of making money on the radio evaporated.

On the other hand, some encouraging news came from Arna Bontemps, who assured Hughes that the Rosenwald Fund was going to fund his request for a grant. The previous December, Hughes had proposed writing a series of one-act plays featuring black heroes, which could be dramatized by high schools, colleges, and amateur theatrical groups. These plays would fill a need for inspirational figures and messages in literature for black youths, Hughes wrote in his application. He made a similar argument in an essay he wrote for the *Crisis* called "The Need for Heroes." Criticizing both Wright's *Native Son* and his own play *Mulatto*, he argued that black writers should stop expending their creative energy on "tragedies of frustration and weakness." Instead, their writing should celebrate black achievements. They should write the kind of books that would make readers feel pride in their race (qtd. in *LLH* II: 14–15). He appeared not to recognize the irony of his directing against other black writers' charges that echoed those once made against his own first books of poetry.

The grant began in June and offered some much-needed financial relief. As with the Guggenheim Fellowship he had won in 1936, however, Hughes at first gave into the temptation to take the money without getting immediately to work on the project that was ostensibly being funded. Instead, he spent some time in Phoenix where he outlined several short stories, and then went to Los Angeles to try once more to break into the movie business.

He met with William Grant Still, who reported no success in finding a producer for their opera *Troubled Island*. Hughes and another writer, Charles Leonard, proposed two different ideas for scripts to Columbia Pictures, but both were rejected. Hughes returned to Carmel and wrote seven stories based on the outlines he had done in Phoenix, but Leiber had some difficulties placing them. It was November before he finally headed to Chicago to start work on his Rosenwald Fund project.

In Chicago, Bontemps arranged for Hughes to stay rent free at the Good Shepherd Community Center, which proclaimed itself "The World's Largest Settlement House." Horace Cayton, who directed the center, and his wife, Irma, became good friends of Hughes, who quickly volunteered to start a drama group at the center.

During the month he spent in Chicago, Hughes worked primarily on a play called *The Sun Do Move*, which was an expansion of his earlier effort, "Sold Away." The drama focused on a slave who is sold away from his family and struggles to secure their freedom and his own. At the conclusion he joins the Union Army. Hughes decided to make this the first production of the new drama group, the Skyloft Players. Although this wasn't the project he had promised the Rosenwald Fund, he hoped that they would extend his fellowship on the strength of this work.

Meanwhile, in early December, the proofs of *Shakespeare in Harlem* arrived. Hughes was pleased with them, even though he had been unable to change his publisher's mind about the illustrations. However, he was horrified a month later when he saw that the dust jacket of his book was illustrated with dice and wishbones, which Hughes saw as tacky, stereotypical symbols of black culture, although the people at Knopf could not understand his complaint. In any case, it was too late to change the cover before the February publication date. (When protests did come in, Knopf agreed to a new jacket design should the book go into a second printing.)

December also brought the attack on Pearl Harbor, and the United States soon found itself at war with both Japan and Germany. One of the heroes of Pearl Harbor was a black messman, Dorie Miller. During the attack on the *Arizona*, Miller commandeered a machine-gun and shot down four Japanese planes. Hughes celebrated his actions in a poem called "Jim Crow's Last Stand" (*CP* 299). In this poem, Hughes optimistically predicted that the war would bring about the end of segregation. Blacks and whites would fight together for democracy, and, as a result, the status of blacks would change. The armed forces were still segregated, and until 1941, when a segregated Negro squadron was formed by the Air Corps, only the Army allowed blacks to fight and serve as officers.

After Hughes moved to Harlem in mid-December, staying first with old friends Toy and Emerson Harper and then at the Theresa Hotel, he became increasingly involved with the war effort, writing some radio scripts for the Office of Civilian Defense. For these he received no payment even though he later found out that white writers who contributed to the program were paid. One of Hughes's radio scripts was rejected as too controversial. Titled "Brothers," it concerned the racism faced by a black sailor returning home from duty. Hughes was discouraged by this further proof that radio, like the film industry, was not open to realistic depictions of black life and concerns.

Hughes's Rosenwald Fellowship was not renewed, but he did complete *The Sun Do Move*, which premiered in late April at the Good Shepard

Community Center. Although the play continued its run for a month, Hughes, who had moved back to Chicago in February, now returned again to Harlem and moved in with the Harpers. He joined another war-related project, accepting a position on the Writers' War Committee advisory board where he was the only black member. Hughes offered some literary contributions to the "Treasury Star Parade Program," through which the Treasury Department promoted the purchase of war bonds. In addition to more than a dozen poems and a short script about folk heroes, Hughes submitted the script of "Brothers," which was again rejected although the other work was accepted.

Hughes was not paid for these written contributions to the war effort nor for various broadcasts he made, so he began trying his hand at song-writing in hopes of writing a popular hit that would make him financially successful. Needing a composer, he collaborated with Emerson Harper. Harper was a musician who had just become the first black man in the CBS studio orchestra. Together, they wrote songs including "Freedom Road," and "That Eagle of the U.S.A." On another song "Go-and-Get-the-Enemy Blues," Hughes collaborated with W.C. Handy and Clarence Jones.

Though fame and fortune eluded him, he continued to work on songs after he accepted an invitation to spend the summer of 1942 at Yaddo, a colony for writers and artists. All told, various lyrics written between 1926 and 1942 would earn him $400 in 1942 from the American Society of Composers, Authors and Publishers (*LLH* II: 49).

Hughes planned a lecture tour for the fall of 1942 but was called to register for the draft in October. He did so, but not without also registering a protest against segregation in the armed forces, which he decried as "contrary to the letter and spirit of the Constitution and damaging to the morale" of both American blacks and "millions of our darker allies" (qtd. in *LLH* II: 53). On November 9, he was granted a 60-day deferment so that he could complete his lecture tour, but the number of appearances was scaled down.

During his tour he emphasized that the war provided an opportunity to fight both fascism and segregation. His predominantly black audiences were receptive and Hughes faced no pickets. In December, he returned to New York at the behest of the draft board. By this time he had also begun a new venture. At the end of October, Hughes had accepted an offer to write a weekly 1,000-word column for the *Chicago Defender*. The column appeared on Thursdays, beginning on November 21, 1942. He christened the column "From Here to Yonder," and included among the subjects of his first columns were an encounter with Josephine Baker in Paris, a childhood reminiscence, a tribute to the musician W.C. Handy, and a scathing editorial about the Red Cross's policy of keeping blood donated by blacks separate from the supply of "white" blood. In February, men over 38 years were exempted from the draft and Hughes was spared the ordeal of serving in the segregated armed forces, though he would not forget the plight of those who did serve. In an essay, "My America," and in a pamphlet of poems that he published in 1943 called *Jim Crow's Last Stand,* Hughes avowed both his patriotism and his protest against racism. For a "colored American," wrote Hughes in "My America," "the phrase about liberty and justice does not apply fully" (500).

He was also commissioned by the National Urban League to write a prose poem to be recited to orchestral accompaniment by the Broadway star Paul Muni. Hughes called his piece "Freedom's Plow," and in it he celebrates the dream and promise of America and urges both black and white Americans to keep striving to realize the common dream. With a score by Dean Dixon, the poem was read on the radio on March 15, 1943.

Throughout 1943, Hughes pursued a variety of genres. However, the primary means by which Hughes took his message about the need for black Americans both to support the war effort and to seize the opportunity to prod their country to live up to her ideals where race was concerned was through the pages of his *Chicago Defender* column and through the voice of a character named Jesse B. Semple.

Semple, also known as Simple, was a folk character whom Hughes's readers soon embraced, a few to the point of taking him for a real person and sending letters to him at the *Chicago Defender.* In the first column, he is simply introduced as the narrator's "Simple Minded Friend" and the unnamed narrator appears to be Hughes himself. The column consists of a recounted conversation in a Harlem bar. The narrator teases his friend about his reluctance to get up early and warns him that he will have to give up sleeping in when he joins the army to fight Hitler. When Simple expresses his pain at being "Jim Crowed" while wearing his country's uniform, the narrator argues that beating Hitler is "helping to beat Jim Crow." Semple agrees but points out that he would like to defeat "Jim Crow" first, since he must live with the effects of segregation in his daily life.

The "Simple Minded Friend" reappeared in the next two columns and then again several weeks later. Ultimately, he would appear in about a quarter of Hughes's columns. Hughes continued to present these as recounted dialogues enjoyed over a beer. The first few focused on the attitude of blacks towards the war, and Hughes continued to push the message that fighting fascism abroad was the best way for blacks to bring about change in America. But gradually the columns featuring Hughes's Simple Minded Friend began to explore other aspects of life in Harlem. The character acquired a name, a past, and a complicated present; Jesse B. Semple grew up in Virginia and then escaped the South for Harlem. He is originally married to Isabel, whom he eventually divorces, and he juggles two girl friends—Joyce, who becomes his second wife, and Zarita, the troublemaker whom he cannot resist. He is also harassed by his domineering landlady. He complains about life in Harlem and forcefully voices his resentment of the white world, but remains full of good humor. The narrator, too, gradually emerges as a fictional character, who speaks in formal, proper English rather than with Simple's more colorful phrases and who is named Boyd. Boyd frequently criticizes his friend, but seeks out his company and at times seems a little envious of his friend's zest for life. Hughes continued to write columns featuring Simple for more than 20 years, and, in 1950, began to collect the columns into a series of books. This popular creation proved a way for Hughes to reach a wider black audience than ever before, as readers who did not care for poetry looked eagerly forward to the next Simple column.

In addition to the *Chicago Defender* columns, Hughes was a regular contributor for the magazine *Common Ground*. Hughes wrote a humorous and controversial essay called "White Folks Do the Funniest Things" which presented segregation as absurd, and a more serious piece titled "What Should We Do About the South?," which urged the necessity of abolishing segregation in order to unite the nation in defense of democracy. He also protested the treatment of Japanese Americans who were sent to relocation camps, and pledged his support for the Indian quest for independence from Britain. In June, he agreed to be one of the sponsors for an "Emergency Committee to Save the Jews of Europe."

Hughes planned a brief reading tour in April to help raise the funds to pay his taxes. For the first time in several years, he was met by protestors when he arrived at the auditorium to give his first lecture at Wayne University in Detroit. The picketers were supporters of the America First Party, which opposed the war and denounced Hughes as both an atheist and a Communist. A police escort got Hughes safely past the picket line and he proceeded to give a rousing speech defending freedom of speech and denouncing the use of religion "to beat down Jews [and] Negroes, and to persecute other minority groups" (qtd. in *LLH* II: 69). The audience rose to its feet at the end of Hughes's presentation, and he encountered no more protests as his tour continued with six engagements in Canada and several in Ohio and Pennsylvania. Two inexpensive pamphlets, the long poem *Freedom's Plow*, and the collection *Jim Crow's Last Stand*, were offered for sale at most appearances. While in Pennsylvania, Hughes attended commencement exercises at his alma mater, Lincoln University, which granted him an honorary doctorate of letters.

As Hughes's tour was winding down, racial violence was heating up in several U.S. cities. Most of the incidents took place when the shortage of labor caused by the draft led to blacks being hired for jobs normally reserved for whites. White workers often responded by striking, and riots followed. In July, Hughes received an invitation from New York's Mayor Fiorello La Guardia to contribute to a series of radio programs entitled "Unity at Home—Victory Abroad." The goal of the program would be to foster civic pride and a spirit of cooperation among New York's citizens in the hope that the racial violence that had erupted in other cities would not spread there.

Hughes agreed to contribute a few scripts, but in the meantime a riot began on the first of August when a white policeman shot a black man who had intervened in an argument between the officer and a black woman. The woman, named Margie Polite, then ran out into the street crying erroneously that the policeman had killed the man who had come to her defense. Her cries inflamed the crowd, starting a riot that would claim five lives and result in about 400 injuries and five million dollars' worth of property damage (*LLH* II: 75). While many middle-class blacks felt only outrage and shame at the riots, and black leaders publicly condemned them, Hughes felt some sympathy with the rioters. He expressed these feelings in a playful poem, the "Ballad of Margie Polite," which proclaims August 1 as "MARGIE'S DAY" (*CP* 282–83) and credits Margie with keeping "the Mayor— / and Walter White— / And everybody / Up all night!" More seriously, Hughes pointed out in letters to friends that progress on racial issues often followed such uprisings. Nevertheless, he did heed the call of the Writers' War Board for material that might help to ease the situation. "In the Service of My Country," a short radio play about blacks and whites working together on the Alaska-Canada Highway, was highly praised and broadcast right away. The second play, "Private Jim Crow," which revealed the daily indignities faced by blacks in the armed forces, was perceived as too controversial, much as "Brothers" had been rejected a few years earlier.

In October, Hughes broke through the color line himself by becoming the first black writer to be offered membership in PEN, an international writers' organization. A short speaking tour in the late fall with stops in Kentucky, Tennessee, North Carolina, and Virginia left Hughes excited about changes he saw in the South. His audiences seemed less passive, more eager to confront and overcome segregation. Hughes made his own contribution on a national radio program in February 1944. Broadcast by NBC, the program was *America's Town Meeting of the Air* and the topic of the day was "Let's Face the Race Question." Each side of the debate was represented by both a black and a white speaker. Hughes and Carey McWilliams, the author of *Brothers Under the Skin*, took the position that segregation must end, while John Temple Graves II, author of *The Fighting South*, and James E. Sheperd, the president of North Carolina College of Negroes, defended segregation. Hughes eloquently and calmly made his case while Graves and Sheperd appeared defensive. Hughes pointed out that blacks were not asking for special rights or to take anything away from whites, but merely to be recognized as Americans entitled to the same rights that whites enjoyed. He mocked the white fear that intermarriage would become common as soon as blacks were granted political rights and pointed to the Soviet Union as proof that racial problems could be resolved. He was deluged with appreciative letters after the show aired as well as some hate mail from those who wished him back to Russia or Africa (*LLH* II: 83–84).

Hughes's performance on the radio program was probably instrumental in helping Max Leiber negotiate a speaking tour for Hughes with Feakins, Inc., a prominent speakers bureau. Hughes became their first black speaker, and the radio show provided valuable publicity for his tour. As part of this tour, Hughes visited Fort Huachuca in Arizona, the country's largest black army post. Impressed by the courage and discipline of the soldiers, both men and women, Hughes celebrated them in long articles for the *Chicago Defender*.

Although his hectic touring schedule had left him little time for creative work, Hughes found himself relatively prosperous. Indeed, in April 1944 he noted that for the first time in his life, his bank balance topped $1,000 (*LLH* II: 86). Hughes resolved to spend some of that money to buy back the rights to the five books he had published with Knopf before 1941, which he had sold to them for $400 out of financial desperation three years earlier. The firm agreed to reinstate his rights as of May 1, 1944, and did not require him to repay the $400 as long as he agreed that no royalties would be due on the sales of the books during the period that Knopf had owned them. Recovering his rights gave Hughes a sense of triumph and seemed to be proof that he had overcome the dark days of 1940.

Chapter 17

"RED-TINGED POET"

Perhaps conscious of having neglected his plans to write inspiring plays for black high school students, Hughes undertook a different project aimed at young people in the fall of 1944. He planned a tour of schools in which he would address the students and read his poems at a school assembly, followed by lunch in the cafeteria and classroom visits. The tour was sponsored by the Common Council for American Unity and the magazine *Common Ground*. Hughes's goal was twofold. He wanted to make the black students, many of whom attended schools with no black teachers, feel pride in their race. He also wanted to help the white students, some of whom attended all-white or nearly all-white schools, learn to see African Americans as fellow human beings who could be articulate and intelligent.

Just before the tour was to begin, on October 3, 1944, Congressman J. B. Matthews brought up Hughes's name in a speech to the House of Representatives Special Committee on Un-American Activities. In this speech and in another two days later, Matthews labeled Hughes as a prominent Communist Party member who advocated dangerous, radical views.

The focus of this committee, which had been in existence for several years, was to investigate subversive propaganda. This was actually the third time Hughes's name had been brought to the attention of the committee. In 1938, Hughes had been branded a Communist poet, and excerpts from two poems were read into the Congressional Record: "Goodbye Christ" which Hughes had since repudiated, and "One More 'S' in the U.S.A.," which Hughes had written in 1934. Furthermore, in

1941 Matthews asserted falsely in a committee hearing that Hughes was not only a member of the Communist Party but had run for office on the party ticket.

Nothing had come of either incident, but in this instance, the committee was aggressively attempting to establish that the National Citizens' Political Action Committee was a Communist front organization. Hughes was one of the integrated organization's 141 members. Matthews was trying to make his case against the group and its chairman, Sidney Hillman, by showing that the members of the organization had ties to the Communist Party itself or to other groups that had already been classified as subversive by the U.S. Attorney General. Hughes figured prominently in this line of argument because he was linked with 12 of these groups and had published in venues deemed subversive. Matthews argued that Hillman's association with a poet so avowedly Communist as Hughes was proof of Hillman's own Communist leanings. Once again, Matthews read from the same two poems, arguing that they were typical of Hughes's work.

As a result of this presentation of Hughes, the poet was attacked by a conservative columnist for the *New York Sun*, and administrators from several high schools he was scheduled to visit cancelled his appearances. Hughes responded by once again distancing himself from "Goodbye Christ," which he called a failed satire on the abuse of religion. Privately though, he fumed that the attacks were racially motivated. Stung by the cancellations, he offered to withdraw from the tour, but the head of the Council would not hear of it. The Council issued a vigorous defense of Hughes and some of the schools reconsidered. The tour began as scheduled on October 16. It was meaningful for Hughes because it allowed him to carry to young people his message that the current war to preserve democracy abroad was also a very welcome opportunity to extend democracy at home.

Meanwhile, Hughes, who had not been actively involved with many leftist organizations for some time—though several continued to use his name—took the precaution of declining to attend or be involved in the Southern Negro Youth Conference in the fall of 1944. From time to time, however, he still quietly asserted his admiration of the Soviet Union. Hostility towards the Soviet Union had been mollified by the Soviet army's contributions to the Allies, and Hughes's poems celebrating Soviet military heroism in the war effort were not criticized. The extended tour that Hughes took in the spring of 1945 under Feakins management drew appreciative crowds and no pickets, and it seemed that once again political attacks on Hughes had blown over.

With the end of the war in Europe, Hughes wrote a column for the *Defender* praising the Soviets' moral superiority on issues of racial justice. Unlike Washington or London, Hughes wrote, "Moscow will support NONE of Hitler's policies in Berlin" ("The Fall of Berlin" 137). In November 1945, the FBI decided to remove his name from a list of important Communist figures, determining that there was no evidence of serious involvement in Communist activities (*LLH* II: 140).

Hughes continued to keep a low political profile in the years following the war. He proposed a new poetry collection to Knopf, which would feature poems less explicitly racial or political than those in any other he had composed. This collection, which he titled *Fields of Wonder,* would be a gathering of lyric poems, some written as far back as the early twenties, although, as Rampersad notes, some critics did not recognize this and ironically praised the volume as the work of a more mature Hughes (*LLH* II: 131). Many poems were about nature or about the poet's own sense of isolation. There are, of course, poems that feature black people, but less often as speaking subjects than as objects of aesthetic appreciation. The book, published in the spring of 1947, received modest praise in some quarters and mild criticism in others from readers who felt that, as the *People's World* lamented, Hughes had "abandoned his origins and sources of strength" in turning away from his more typical racial and political subject matter (qtd. in *LLH* II: 131).

Perhaps Hughes himself agreed with this assessment on some level because around the time that *Fields of Wonder* was being reviewed, he began work on another collection featuring poems with racial themes. When Blanche Knopf was less than enthusiastic about bringing out another collection so soon after *Fields of Wonder,* he sent this manuscript to Arna Bontemps for feedback rather than to Carl Van Vechten or Knopf. (Nevertheless, Knopf would eventually publish this collection in the fall of 1948.) Hughes had already endured other rejections from Knopf that had strained their relationship. First, in 1946 she dismissed both his plans to translate some of Nicolás Guillén's poems and his idea for a collection of sketches featuring Simple from his *Chicago Defender* columns. Next, she was noncommittal about a proposed anthology of African American poetry to be edited by Hughes and Bontemps. Hughes began to look elsewhere. An editor at Doubleday offered a $1,000 advance for their anthology. But Hughes had less luck with the Simple sketches. Although the character was enormously popular and Hughes had published an essay about him in the winter 1945 issue of *Phylon,* so far he had been unable to turn Simple into a commercial success other than getting the *Chicago De-*

fender to raise his pay by $10 a week. For a time he had hoped that a black publisher, John H. Johnson, might bring out an inexpensive paperback edition, but Johnson changed his mind when Hughes asked for a small advance. At Current Books, Bernard Perry made an offer on the Simple book and offered what Hughes termed a "splendid advance" but asked for additional chapters and revisions that Hughes found preposterous. He refused to sign the contract (Nichols 217).

Hughes was not compelled to give in to Perry's demands because of his financial success as the lyricist for *Street Scene*, a triumph to be discussed in the following chapter. This income also enabled him to cut back on lectures. Instead, he took a position as a Visiting Professor of Creative Writing at Atlanta University for the spring 1947 semester. While Hughes found university life pleasant, humiliating experiences with segregation marred his stay. Meanwhile, the flow of money from *Street Scene* helped finance the use of several part-time secretaries. Hughes worked on *One-Way Ticket* (the new collection of poems) and his anthology with Bontemps. On a trip to Jamaica in the fall of 1947, he made several contacts with young Caribbean writers whose work he planned to include in the anthology.

After two relatively smooth years, Hughes was unprepared when, in late 1947, controversy surfaced following a Thanksgiving Day address he delivered to the convention of the American Education Fellowship, a progressive teachers' organization. An article on the front page of the [New York] *Journal American*, questioned the educators' choice of a Communist Party member as keynote speaker. This in turn inspired more attacks in newspaper columns and by radio commentators repeating all the old charges. When Hughes embarked on a speaking tour in January 1948, he found himself repeatedly having to assure his audiences that he was not a Communist and had no intentions of advocating the overthrow of the U.S. government.

Meanwhile, several organizations, including the Knights of Columbus, the American Legion, and a group of supporters of Gerald L. K. Smith, combined forces to try to persuade the sponsors of Hughes's lectures to cancel his appearances. Some sponsors, concerned about the rumors of Hughes's Communist affiliation, inquired of the FBI. The bureau's replies declined to provide direct evidence yet implied the rumors were true. In Springfield, Illinois, the NAACP, the Urban League, and the YWCA voted to cancel a scheduled talk for fear that protests would become violent and lead to a race riot. A private school near Chicago cancelled his lecture after an article in the *Chicago Tribune* warned that a "red-tinged poet" had been invited to speak, inflaming parental concerns (qtd. in

LLH II: 142). After local newspapers editorialized against him in Akron, Ohio, Hughes could not find a hall open to him.

On April 1, 1948, Hughes was denounced in the Senate. Senator Albert W. Hawkes of New Jersey claimed to have attended a lecture by Hughes in a New Jersey church. According to Hawkes, Hughes made no mention of religion but instead used the pulpit to attack the United States and praise the Soviet Union. Then, once again, the poems "Goodbye Christ" and "One More 'S' in the U.S.A." were read aloud as damning evidence against Hughes.

Doggedly Hughes continued the tour, but even after he reached California his opponents continued to attack and denounce him and to use intimidation to persuade sponsors and venues to cancel his appearances. Hughes explained his position over and over in newspaper interviews and his own column. He was not a Communist, but he respected the Soviet Union for its fair treatment of racial minorities. His poems were not dangerous, and attacks on him were really prompted by racial prejudice and the desire to derail progress on civil rights for blacks. Nevertheless, the whole experience was demoralizing, and Hughes decided to take a season off from the lecture circuit.

He returned to New York in June, in time to participate in the final preparations for moving with Toy and Emerson Harper into a house on East 127th Street. Emerson Harper had purchased it the previous December with the money Hughes had earned from *Street Scene*. The deed to the house was eventually put in the names of Hughes and both Harpers. Langston had a two-room suite on the top floor of the large house where seven boarders as well Hughes and the Harpers lived. Hughes had insisted that his new home be in Harlem and, except for some traveling, he would remain there for the rest of his life. He and the Harpers moved into the house in July 1948, and the roomers were established that fall.

Although it is true that Hughes was practically forced off the lecture circuit in 1948, this had the advantage of giving him the chance to immerse himself in Harlem and his work. In a burst of creative energy he produced a book-length poem over the course of a week, which he called *Montage of a Dream Deferred*.

Just as his older poems were linked to the sounds of black music in spirituals, and especially, the blues, the poems in this book attempt to incorporate recent innovations in jazz known as be-bop. Excited, and recognizing it as his best work in some time, Hughes shared the manuscript with both Bontemps and Van Vechten, who were equally enthusiastic. However he hesitated to offer the manuscript to Knopf. He sought out collaborators, sending a copy to Jacob Lawrence, an artist he had hired at his own expense to illustrate *One-Way Ticket* and another to Harold Swanson, a composer. Meanwhile several of the poems were offered to various magazines, but none accepted. (Later, at the end of 1949, he did offer the book to Knopf and was probably not surprised by her rejection. Eventually another firm, Henry Holt, accepted the manuscript.)

As of 1948, no publisher had yet accepted the Simple manuscript. Hughes was aware that stand-up comedians had started to "borrow" material from the Simple columns in their routines, and, in frustration, he considered trying to develop it into a radio program. What kept him from pursuing it was a concern that Simple's comedy might be too controversial for the airwaves.

Work on the anthology, *The Poetry of the Negro*, was proving tedious and exhausting. The book was intended to include poetry both by and about blacks, but some West Indian writers feared being labeled "Negro" and were reluctant to be included. Hughes found the work of securing permissions and writing or obtaining biographical notes for each included author to be tiresome. Nevertheless Hughes persevered, committed to bringing more attention to the work of black poets.

When the anthology appeared at the end of 1948, it sold well, but because of the cost of permissions, earned no money beyond the initial advance for some time. Reviews were often favorable, but certain— sometimes contradictory—criticisms were advanced. Some felt that Caribbean writers should not have been included, while at least one critic argued that the book's weakness was its limited international scope, especially its inclusion of the work of few African writers. Others argued that writing by whites should have been excluded or that more attention should have been given to folklore (*LLH* II: 159).

One-Way Ticket also appeared at year's end. Reviewers were not enthusiastic, several lamenting the apparent simplicity or superficiality of Hughes's work. J. Saunders Redding, who had often reviewed Hughes favorably, pronounced the collection "stale, flat and spiritless" (73). One gratifying review, however, came from David Daiches, who judged that Hughes had succeeded in "project[ing] the living American Negro on the page" (qtd. in *LLH* II: 161). Hughes himself liked several of the protest poems well enough to include them again in his final volume, *The Panther and the Lash*, nearly 20 years later.

For the second spring in a row, Hughes accepted a teaching position, this time at the University of Chicago's Laboratory School. Langston would earn $2,000 as a visiting lecturer on poetry, telling stories with kindergarteners, helping eighth graders write autobiography and publish a literary magazine, and lecturing high school students on "The Negro in

American Poetry." Hughes found the students warm and receptive but the schedule strenuous. He never again accepted a teaching position despite later offers from both Atlanta University and the Hampton Institute.

Just before leaving to take up the teaching position, he received the welcome news that at last a publisher, Simon and Schuster, had accepted the Simple manuscript. Maria Leiper would be his editor, and from the first they enjoyed a far warmer and more harmonious relationship than he had ever had with Blanche Knopf. With Leiper's guidance Hughes delivered the final manuscript of *Simple Speaks His Mind* to his publisher at the end of the summer.

National anxiety over the threat of Communism and a possible atomic war with the Soviet Union continued to grow. In April, following the notorious Waldorf-Astoria Conference of the National Council of the Arts, Sciences and Professions, Hughes was depicted in *Life* magazine as one of 50 prominent Americans who lent support to Communism, either deliberately or as a result of political naïveté, by supporting the conference. Hughes was a member of the Council and was listed as a sponsor of the conference, but there is no record of his actual participation. In fact, he declined requests to participate and even at one point asked the Council not to use his name. Nevertheless he appeared on *Life*'s list and soon afterward *Reader's Digest* printed excerpts from a radio broadcast attacking Hughes. Once again, testimony in Congressional hearings included bringing up Hughes's name in order to question the politics of those who were in any way associated with him.

In this environment, Hughes was understandably cautious; nevertheless, he did take a political risk in a February 5, 1949, *Chicago Defender* column. He denounced the trial of 12 suspected Communists accused of supporting the overthrow of the government, and called on his black readers to recognize that whatever their political leanings, their rights were also potentially at risk. "If the twelve Communists are sent to jail," wrote Hughes, making an analogy with Hitler's Germany, "in a little while they will send Negroes to jail simply for being Negroes and to concentration camps just for being colored" ("A Portent" 184). Hughes also agreed to a request of the Communist Party of New York to reprint his column. It was a brave step and one that would be used against him four years later when he was called to face Senator Joe McCarthy.

Chapter 18

"FOOLING AROUND WITH THE THEATRE"

Despite the fiasco of *Mule Bone*, the sensationalizing of *Mulatto*, the disappointment of *Way Down South*, and his inability to interest Hollywood in any of the various other film treatments he had proposed over the years, Hughes felt a persistent attraction to writing for stage and screen. In the 1940s and early 1950s Hughes was involved with several musical theatrical projects for which he wrote the lyrics and in some cases the underlying play: the opera *Troubled Island* (based on his play *Drums of Haiti*), the Broadway show *Street Scene*, and the opera *The Barrier*, based on his play *Mulatto*. Each venture brought him certain troubles, but *Street Scene* also brought a measure of financial success that helped him survive being forced from the lecture circuit in 1948 due to political opposition.

In 1944, Hughes got some encouraging news on one project that had long languished; at last William Grant Still had found a conductor interested in staging *Troubled Island*, written back in 1937. Leopold Stokowski, one of the few conductors to have featured African American principal singers, proposed staging the show at the New York City Center. Hughes met Stokowski in November and was enthusiastic about his plans to use black singers, dancers, and a choir in the production, for at this time few opera venues even allowed any black performers. The only problem was to raise the estimated $30,000 needed to finance the production. Unfortunately, Stokowski soon resigned his position as musical director for the City Center and only $2,000 of donations were received. For several years the City Center continued to profess some interest in staging the opera but to insist on more private funding, leading Still to announce in June 1947 that he was withdrawing the opera and to demand that the donations be returned. The Center complied, to Hughes's chagrin, for he had been looking forward to its production. Still then offered the opera to the Metropolitan, but they declined, explaining that they could not do the production since their company had no black singers.

Belatedly, in the fall of 1948, the City Center had a change of heart and began to prepare a production for the following spring. This unexpected success prompted Still to demand that Hughes recognize his wife Vera Arvey as the co-author of the libretto. To Hughes this was a sudden and surprising claim, though he recognized that Arvey had indeed written some of the lyrics. While Hughes was in Spain in 1937, Still made some changes to the score. With Hughes unavailable, Arvey had supplied new lines to fit the music. Conceding this, Hughes was willing to grant her a share of the royalties, but insisted that these contributions did not amount to co-authorship. The rift caused by Hughes's refusal to bow to all of Still's demands was never really healed, though the production went ahead.

The opera premiered on March 30, 1949, at the City Center. Even though white singers preformed the prominent roles, several African Americans had roles in the chorus or as dancers. Hughes was proud that his was the first opera written by blacks to be produced in America. Despite a warm audience reaction, however, the reviewers were hostile. The limited budget was apparent in the costumes, and the quality of the dancing was criticized, but the main complaint of the reviewers was with the music. It was not original. Still did not create his own style, but instead echoed the work of a variety of other composers (*LLH* II: 166). Hughes confided to Van Vechten that he felt the opera lacked "a really big musical moment" (Bernard 257) and, in turn, Van Vechten criticized the music, direction, casting, and anti-climactic ending (Bernard 257–58) despite professing to admire the work overall. For his part, Still blamed Hughes, believing that his notoriety as a suspected Communist was the cause of the negative reviews.

In August 1945, Hughes plunged into another project when he received an unexpected telegram from Elmer Rice. Rice was a successful white playwright whom Hughes knew casually. In 1929, Rice's play *Street Scene* won a Pulitzer Prize and had since been made into a film. Hughes knew and admired both versions. Rice had recently decided to collaborate with Kurt Weill in creating a musical version of the play. They invited Hughes to join them as the lyricist for the project. As Rampersad points out, it was quite a startling proposal in the 1940s for two successful white artists to ask a black man to collaborate on a Broadway play about whites. However, as all three of the participants agreed, Hughes was in some ways an obvious choice. They sought someone who knew and understood the lives of the poor, and could create poetry from their experiences, using everyday language (*LLH* II: 109).

After his trial lyrics to two songs met with the approval of Weill and Rice, Hughes was given an advance of $500 and began working steadily to complete additional lyrics. The terms of the agreement were that Weill and Rice would make a decision by November 15 on whether to use his contributions. If they dismissed him, he would receive another $250, earning a total of $750 for two months' work. On the other hand, if they decided to use his lyrics, he would receive 2 percent of the box-office gross and 20 percent of the film rights (*LLH* II: 110).

Hughes went only grudgingly to fulfill various reading engagements, devoting every spare moment to the *Street Scene* project. His hard work paid off when his lyrics won him the job. Throughout the winter Hughes continued to work with Rice and Weill, sometimes forced to try to mediate between the composer and playwright when artistic differences arose. One black character, a janitor, was added to the show. When the songs for the first act were completed, Hughes embarked on a six-week reading tour of the western United States before coming back to marathon sessions on *Street Scene*. Interest from Hollywood increased the show's budget, and Dwight Deere Wiman had signed on as the producer. Rehearsals would start in the fall with a Broadway opening set for December.

Up until rehearsals began, Rice, Weill, and Hughes continued to tinker with the show, dropping some songs and adding others. Hughes was disappointed when two of the three songs he wrote for the role of the black janitor were eliminated, seeing it as further evidence that Broadway was not truly open to featuring the stories of blacks. The play opened for a trial run in Philadelphia on December 16, and received only one favorable review.

The main complaint of the other reviewers was that the play was too long, contained too many songs, and tried to encompass too many different genres. Privately Hughes concurred, writing to Bontemps that if only he were in a position to take charge of the script, rather than merely being the lyricist, he could attempt to fix the problem, which he diagnosed as shifting awkwardly between the modes of opera, musical comedy, and drama (Nichols 213).

As it was, Hughes's ability to work with Rice and Weill was hampered by the refusal of the hotel where they were lodged to admit black guests, though once, when he entered the dining room with them anyway, he was served without objection. Several songs were dropped and the rest shortened so that the play's running time had been cut by a full half-hour by the time the three-week run ended with the production $170,000 in debt (*LLH* II: 125).

With some trepidation on the part of everyone involved, the play opened on Broadway on January 9, 1947. Despite the bad weather, the house was full and the play generated an enthusiastic audience response. The reviews were enthusiastic, often offering particular praise to Hughes's lyrics. Soon Hughes was receiving regular royalty payments and was fielding inquiries about other Broadway projects. *Street Scene* eventually closed in May after nearly 150 performances.

As if to reinforce Hughes's growing belief that, because of its collaborative nature, writing for theater always leads to disputes over royalties, Hughes received an unwelcome demand from Elmer Rice in August 1947 for co-credit as lyricist on the sheet music for *Street Scene* and half of his royalties on both the sheet music and the recordings. Remembering his own past struggles with Hurston, Hughes tried to be fair. He understood Rice's contention that in some cases the song lyrics were similar to the words of Rice's script, and he did not deny that Rice had made a few other suggestions which he had incorporated; still he insisted the bulk of the lyrics were his alone and felt that Rice's demands were excessive. He declined to credit Rice as a co-author of the lyrics for the entire score but agreed to give him credit on seven individual songs. He proposed allowing Rice as much as two-thirds of the royalties on the published music but only 30 percent of the more lucrative recording royalties. Rice proposed 40 percent and then raised additional demands, prompting Hughes to leave the matter in the hands of his lawyer while he took a month-long trip to Jamaica. To Hughes's relief, an amicable settlement was eventually reached.

Among the many inquiries prompted by the success of *Street Scene*, Hughes had been particularly interested in a letter from Jan Meyerowitz, a young composer who had recently immigrated from Europe. Meyerowitz wrote that he had set some of Hughes's poems to music and would be interested in meeting him to discuss a possible collaboration. He proposed creating an opera from Hughes's short story "Father and Son," not realizing that it had already had a run on Broadway as the play *Mulatto*. The existence of *Mulatto* only increased Meyerowitz's interest in an operatic treatment of the story featuring modern music. As a Jew who had been forced to flee Germany, Meyerowitz identified with the story of rebellion against the pain and injustice of prejudice and discrimination. Soon he had written a first act that impressed Hughes. After his return from Jamaica, Hughes learned that Meyerowitz had completed the score.

Given the controversial nature of the subject matter, however, it was difficult to get from there to an actual production. After nearly two years, Joel Spector, a musician and former assistant stage director at the Metropolitan Opera, expressed an interest in bringing the Meyerowitz and Hughes version of *Mulatto* to Broadway. As an interim step he proposed a 10-day production by the Theatre Associates of Columbia University in January 1950. Felix Brentano would be the director, and he suggested that the title be changed to *The Barrier*, so that the audience would not entertain preconceptions based on the sensationalized version that had appeared years earlier.

Brentano found the first act too short and requested a prologue. Hughes complied and Meyerowitz set it to music, but Brentano disliked the music and requested that Meyerowitz try again. The second attempt pleased the director, but he now complained that the overture needed to be rewritten so that it would not clash with the prologue. Under increasing tension, Meyerowitz made the changes and the show went into rehearsals at the end of November.

The premiere of the show at Columbia University on January 18, 1950, brought laudatory reviews and revived hopes of a Broadway production. Although Kurt Weill was skeptical, praising the show but warning that there was no audience for this kind of theater, Hughes's backers were encouraged by the reviews. Another producer, Michael Meyerberg, joined forces with Spector to work on bringing the play to Broadway, and they offered Hughes a small advance of $250. Meyerowitz was eager to continue the collaboration as well, even though he experienced hostility from some who wondered why he would willingly work with a suspected Communist (*LLH* II: 177).

That spring, Hughes made various changes to the libretto while struggling at a variety of other projects, trying to raise much-needed funds to pay his living expenses and the salary of his secretary. As in the early 1940s, he hoped for success as a lyricist for popular songs and indeed a few of his songs were recorded by such artists as Burl Ives, Juanita Hill, and the Striders, but none brought him large royalties. Despite repeated efforts, he failed to interest Lena Horne or Mahalia Jackson in recording any of his songs.

During the previous summer, Hughes had accepted a $1,000 advance to work on a musical about the Depression entitled *Just Around the Corner*. He was hired as a replacement lyricist for Charles Bick, writing new lyrics for a score that had largely already been set. Hughes found this difficult but enjoyed working with the composer Joe Sherman and the authors, Abby Mann and Bernard Drew. The play premiered in the summer of 1950 at a vacation town in Maine. Although the audience reaction was good, the reviews were not enthusiastic, and nothing came of producer Mike Todd's brief interest in the show.

With the closing of this play and the disappointing sales of *Simple Speaks His Mind*, Hughes was all the more eager for the Broadway version of *The Barrier* to be a success. Unfortunately, controversy erupted before the show opened for a planned trial run. The production was scheduled to play at the Ford Theater in Baltimore, which segregated black audience members in the balcony. The NAACP threatened to picket the show. Muriel Rahn, the female lead, announced that she would sing as scheduled, but would also join the picket line during the parts of the show when her presence was not required on stage. Hughes followed her lead, claiming he was ready to join the picket line as well. They hoped that the theater owner might be persuaded to change the seating policy in the face of this publicity, but he refused, leading Hughes and his backers to cancel the Baltimore run. The show would play instead in Washington, D.C., but the publicity seemed to backfire. Advance ticket sales were slight and the reviews were hostile. Hughes himself worried that once again his tragic story had become too melodramatic when translated onto the stage. Meyerowitz was critical of the musicians, who, in his opinion, were not skilled enough to handle his music, and also felt that Lawrence Tibbet, an aging white baritone, did not have a strong enough voice to sing the part of the father (*LLH* II: 184). Whatever the reason, *The Barrier*'s Washington run ended after just five performances.

Despite this disappointment, the production was next supposed to open in New York at the Mansfield Theatre, which was owned by Michael Meyerberg. But Meyerberg accepted an irresistible offer from CBS for use of the theater. The production toured suburban theaters in Brooklyn and the Bronx, waiting for another Broadway venue to become available. On November 2, *The Barrier* opened at the Broadhurst Theatre in Manhattan. Two days later, Hughes wrote ruefully to Bontemps that his "worriation" of an opera was closing after only three shows due to "much razzing" from reviewers who attacked the music, as well as other "complications" he declined to enumerate (Nichols 276).

Success on the stage had once again proved elusive. In another letter to Bontemps, Hughes advised his friend against "fooling around with the theatre." Wrote Hughes, "It cripples your soul" (Nichols 244). Though he seemed unable to follow his own advice, his theatrical adventures ended mostly in disappointment or, in the cases when a production was successful, in disputes over royalties. Still, Hughes did not stay away from the stage, going on to write several plays featuring Gospel music in the last two decades of his life.

Chapter 19

FACING DOWN McCARTHY

Short of money and still unable to book a lecture tour because most lecture halls were closed to him, Hughes took on a variety of projects as 1950 approached. One was a commission to write the biography of Samuel Jesse Battle, New York's first black policeman. Hughes interviewed Battle and accepted a $1,500 advance. He also accepted a commission to write an opera set in Pennsylvania, which brought him an advance of $500. For this project he was to work with Elie Siegmeister, a young composer who had set some of Hughes's poems to music. Unfortunately, various other commitments, including the imminent production of his opera *The Barrier* and his work as a lyricist on a musical, *Just Around the Corner*, prevented him from making much progress on either the Battle book or the Pennsylvania opera. Once *Just Around the Corner* closed after a brief Maine run, Hughes did make the time to work with Siegmeister on the preliminary stages of "The Wizard of Altoona," which was to be a love story set in a Pennsylvania coal town. *The Barrier* then called him away from this endeavor, but he returned to both projects intermittently. He complained about pressure from Battle and Siegmeister to finish these works and dodged their calls (Nichols 277, 290; Bernard 267).

Simple Speaks His Mind was published in April 1950 and Hughes anticipated a commercial success. The book was published simultaneously in cloth and paperback bindings, and nearly 14,000 readers placed prepublication orders (mostly of the inexpensive version) (*LLH* II: 178). The text was showered with friendly reviews. Hughes was praised for creating a humorous and believable black narrator, who nevertheless spoke out strongly on racial issues. Yet sales mysteriously lagged after publication.

This, as well as problems in delivery of the copies, led Maria Leiper to wonder if someone were acting to sabotage the sales of the book, so she personally supervised future orders. Although the book eventually sold close to 30,000 copies, it was not the best seller Hughes had anticipated.

Meanwhile, having spent the advances from the Battle project and the Pennsylvania opera, Langston looked for further sources of income. He was hired to write a children's book for Franklin Watts and to contribute to the 25th anniversary exhibit of the Schomberg Collection of Negro History and Literature at the New York Public Library. In response to the announcement that Hughes would write for the exhibit, a local radio personality, Joe Rosenfield, devoted four consecutive nightly broadcasts to denouncing Hughes and reading testimony against him from the HUAC (House Un-American Activities Committee). Unwelcome attention was also focused on Hughes as the result of his inclusion in *Red Channels: A Report of the Communist Influence in Radio and Television*. This pamphlet, by television producer Vincent Harnett and former FBI agent Theodore Kirpatrick, purported to identify 151 individuals with past memberships in various subversive organizations and was mailed without charge to potential employers of those on the list to encourage the blacklisting of these writers, actors, singers, and directors.

Early in 1951, Hughes was able to make a brief reading tour of the South without being harassed by picketers. During this tour, he was dismayed to hear of the arrest of W. E. B. Du Bois for allegedly being an unregistered agent of a foreign government. Du Bois and four white men had formed the Peace Information Center to work for nuclear disarmament. The State Department's view was that such a group must be working for the Soviet Union against U.S. national security interests. The five men were arrested when they refused to sign a statement that they were indeed Soviet agents. Though Du Bois would eventually be acquitted, the experience resulted in a long period of ostracism from much of the black community and was an object lesson for Hughes of a fate he wanted to avoid. Thus, Hughes took pains that spring to minimize any ongoing association between himself and leftist groups such as the National Council of Arts, Sciences and Professions, refusing invitations to speak at several high-profile events, or to add his name to an open letter calling for world peace.

Nevertheless during the week of Du Bois's trial, Hughes spoke out through his column in the *Chicago Defender*. He praised Du Bois's contributions to scholarship, literature, and politics. Condemning the arrest of Du Bois at the behest of "somebody in Washington," he compared it to persecution of other great thinkers and leaders throughout history including Voltaire, Thomas Mann, Socrates, and finally, Christ ("The Accusers'

Names" 188). Some of Du Bois's supporters believed that Hughes's column contributed to the judge's decision to grant a defense motion for a directed acquittal a week later (*LLH* II: 196).

Anti-Communist sentiment continued to mount and touched Hughes's life in several ways. In the spring of 1951, Hughes was selected to receive an award for contributions to the arts by the Philadelphia Fellowship Commission. Given the enormous pressure on members of the entertainment industry to avoid any suggestion of leftist sympathies, Spyros Skouras, the president of Twentieth Century Fox and a fellow award recipient, announced that he would reject his award unless Hughes made a public denunciation of Communism. Outraged, Hughes refused to give such a statement under pressure and the commission withdrew the award. Perhaps a little shaken by this result, he complied with a similar request from Franklin Watts, who asked for a written statement repudiating "Goodbye Christ" and denying affiliation with the Communist Party as a condition of publishing and promoting the children's book he had just completed for them. Max Lieber, Hughes's agent for nearly 20 years, was driven from the United States after Whittaker Chambers fingered him as a communist spy in his autobiography, *Witness*. An attempted reading tour in February 1952 was derailed by protests and threats of violence that led to cancellations throughout Texas.

In March 1953, Hughes received a subpoena commanding him to appear before the Senate Permanent Sub-Committee on Investigations, which was chaired by Senator Joseph McCarthy. Unlike many others called before this committee or the HUAC, Hughes did not want to invoke the Fifth Amendment and refuse to answer questions on the grounds of his right to avoid self-incrimination. In 1947, the so-called Hollywood Ten had challenged the legitimacy of the HUAC to ask questions about their personal relationships and affiliations. They refused to tell whether they were then or had ever been members of the Communist Party, and for this refusal they were found in contempt and jailed. On the other hand, so-called "friendly witnesses" who were willing to testify about themselves and their own past activities and associations would also be pressured to identify others. To avoid this situation, some would plead the Fifth Amendment. "Taking the Fifth," however, would likely be construed as an admission of guilt and could lead to being fired or blacklisted. Hughes was unwilling to risk public opprobrium by refusing to cooperate, and he believed that there was nothing in his writing or beliefs that could really be viewed as subversive. Indeed this might be a chance to clear the air and defuse the right-wing opposition that had periodically threatened his livelihood for over a decade. He hoped that the committee would not ask him for the names of any Communists he might have known, but declared to his lawyer that he actually did not remember any such names and would so inform the committee, if pressured.

Upon receiving the subpoena, Hughes consulted Arthur Spingarn, who referred him to another lawyer, Lloyd Garrison. Hughes met with Garrison to discuss his strategy, but Garrison was unable to accompany him to Washington. Instead he was represented by Frank D. Reeves, a Washington lawyer who had worked with the NAACP. The call for Hughes's testimony was a consequence of a recent campaign by McCarthy against the Voice of America and the State Department's overseas libraries in 63 countries. Hundreds of books were removed from the libraries, reduced to pulp, or actually burned for being subversive. Sixteen books by Hughes were designated as subversive, and he was one of several writers called in to answer questions about his work (*LLH* II: 211).

During his time in Washington, Hughes stayed with Reeves and his family. They rehearsed his testimony and participated in closed sessions with Roy Cohn and some of the other members of the committee where Hughes declared his intention to appear as a friendly witness. In acknowledgment of his cooperation, his more controversial poems would not be read into the record.

Hughes's testimony began with the reading of a five-page prepared statement that was partly based on the one he had previously written for Franklin Watts. The statement began by noting that, unlike poets who wrote about romance and moonlight and nature, he was a poet who wrote about social problems and was therefore bound to be a little controversial. He went on to explain the concept of a dramatic monologue, using examples from several poems. Readers who assumed that the speaker of "Goodbye Christ" was Hughes himself failed to recognize that the "I" of a poem is often a persona. Readers of the poem also frequently missed its irony and took it to be an attack on all religion rather than an attack on abuses of religion such as hucksterism or acceptance of racial segregation. He explained that he had withdrawn the poem from circulation because of so many misguided interpretations of it, but that it had still been used against him to claim falsely that he was a Communist and an atheist. He countered the latter charge by quoting the poem "Ma Lord," a dialect poem in which the speaker praises Jesus as one who knows what it is to work and suffer and who offers the speaker eternal friendship (*CP* 107). Professing admiration for "sincere religionists" like the one in the poem, Hughes then proceeded to deny that he ever was a Communist. He admitted that he had belonged to the "John Reed Club" and other organi-

zations like the "League of American Writers" that were now deemed suspect, but he argued that these groups "belong[ed] to that true American
stream of criticism and of libertarianism which has enriched American
life since its very beginning. . . . I do not believe that the desire for change
and working toward it, is necessarily un-American." He stressed that he
believed in change being achieved through the democratic process, thus
implicitly repudiating violent revolution. He pointed to examples of
works in which he had defended democratic values and criticized those
who claimed to be upholding religion or democracy while pursuing "anti-
Negro and anti-American activities" ("Statement to the Senate"). He
then offered the text of "I Dream a World," an aria from *Troubled Island*,
as reflective of his own political beliefs.

The questioning of Hughes began with Cohn asking if Hughes had ever
believed "in the Soviet form of government" ("Copy" 2–3).[1] Upon
Hughes's affirmative answer, Cohn began to lead him through the standard script for friendly witnesses, who would admit to having been de-
luded by Communist propaganda, explain how they had seen the error of
their ways, condemn the Soviet Union, and praise democracy and the
American system. But Hughes resisted the script a little. He admitted
frankly to sympathizing with Soviet ideology at the time of the Scottsboro
incident and to later becoming disillusioned as a result of the Nazi-Soviet
pact and later incidents of "imperialist aggression" and suppression of free
speech on the part of the Soviet government ("Copy" 3–4). Unlike most
other friendly witnesses, however, he offered no blanket denunciation of
Communism. When Cohn questioned him about his defense of Du Bois,
Hughes stood by it, asserting that he was not writing in favor of Communism but in the interest of preserving civil liberties ("Copy" 3).

Many of the other witnesses called that week refused to cooperate with
the Committee, and Hughes may have felt some qualms about his own cooperation. At some level it seemed to endorse their authority and their
methods. This is particularly clear in those parts of the hearing when
Hughes is pressed to concede the wisdom of the removal of copies of 16 of
his books from State Department libraries. Hughes agreed only that *some*
of these books contain passages that might be said to "follow the Communist line" and suggested that perhaps they could be replaced by more
recent works ("Copy" 8). He also defended an episode from *Simple Speaks
His Mind* that Cohn characterized as "thoroughly ridicul[ing] the activities of the Committee" and undermining their attempts to fight Communism ("Copy" 5). McCarthy pressed Hughes to agree that the book should
be removed from State Department libraries for putting the United States

in a bad light, but Hughes contended that the sketch demonstrated "that we had freedom of the press intact, that we kept the right to satirically comment upon a committee of our government" ("Copy" 7).

When asked at the end of the hearing to help the committee to refute charges in the press that the committee mistreated its witnesses, Hughes replied blandly that he was treated with more courtesy than he expected. When McCarthy joked that Hughes had discovered that the senators "didn't have horns after all," Hughes responded by praising the graciousness of Senator Dirksen but said nothing about the others, and then added, "And the young men who had to interrogate me—of course had to interrogate me. Am I excused now?" ("Closing Testimony" 2). His failure to return McCarthy's pleasantry and his abrupt question reveal his impatience with McCarthy's attempt to convert him into an ally. After his death, a poem published in *The Panther and the Lash* made clear his true feelings about the "Un-American Investigators" of its title. The poem radiates disgust as Hughes accuses the investigators of anti-Semitism and depicts them wallowing in "warm manure" (CP 560).

His testimony pleased many. He received notes of support from Charles S. Johnson, Amy Spingarn, and his editors at Simon and Schuster and Franklin Watts. Both *Time* and the *Amsterdam News* commented favorably on his testimony, and the NAACP stepped in to pay his legal expenses. His testimony at least served the purpose of ending most attacks from the right and depriving those that continued of much of their power to threaten him. Having successfully explained himself to the Senate, Hughes felt that he had put the matter to rest and need no longer fear or even acknowledge his accusers.

Nevertheless, the experience marked him. Strong anti-Soviet sentiment continued for the rest of Hughes's life, and he could never be sure that he would not find himself once more under scrutiny. In the years to come he would bow to pressure from certain of his publishers to exclude material that might be deemed radical or subversive. For example, Hughes agreed to several cuts to his manuscript of a collection of biographical essays on African Americans for young readers that he wrote for Dodd Mead. Under pressure from his editors, he toned down or removed all references to his subjects' experiences of racism. He also eliminated the chapter on Walter White and the NAACP. Despite Hughes's own statement in 1951 that Du Bois was both "a great Negro" and a "great American," in fact "one of the leading men of our century" ("The Accusers' Names" 188), Hughes did not propose a chapter on him for this collection, entitled *Famous American Negroes*. Similarly he left Paul Robeson out of *Famous Negro Music Makers*, a subsequent book for children that Hughes wrote in the mid-fifties.

Sometimes Hughes himself chose these omissions. For instance, the second volume of his autobiography, *I Wonder as I Wander*, though it presented the Soviet Union in a positive light, disappointed some of Hughes's friends on the left by underplaying his radical past. Marie Short, for instance, questioned his failure to write about his involvement with the John Reed Club and the longshoremen's strikes during his time in Carmel (*LLH* II: 260). When making selections for his *Selected Poems*, brought out by Knopf in 1959, Hughes excluded all his radical socialist verse of the 1930s, obscuring the large omission by organizing his verse thematically rather than chronologically.

While interest in the "race question" created a demand for Hughes as a lecturer and an interview subject in the late 1950s, Hughes was careful. He remarked that nobody took much notice when he spoke to black groups, but his appearances before mixed or primarily white audiences drew the ire of conservatives. In 1960, after *Time* magazine, the *New York Times*, and the *New York Post* published erroneous stories alleging that he had met with Fidel Castro during the Cuban leader's visit to New York, Hughes decided to avoid most speaking engagements other than those before black groups. A sign of his rehabilitation in the eyes of the government by the early sixties, however, was that he was sent abroad as a representative of the State Department, and asked to act as host to prominent visitors from Africa.

Note

1. The following discussion is based on a copy of the transcript of Hughes's interrogation and on a transcript of his closing testimony found in the Beinecke Library. Extensive quotations from both documents can be found at Rampersad (*LLH* II: 215–18).

Chapter 20

HUGHES AND THE FREEDOM MOVEMENT

Beginning with his seventh-grade protest against his teacher's segregation of her black students, Hughes was a lifelong opponent of segregation and all expressions of racism. His hopes that fighting for democracy in World War II would inspire white Americans to extend the benefits of democracy to black Americans at home had been largely disappointing. But by the early 1950s, Jim Crow laws and practices were under steady legal attack from the federal government. Court victories, however, were undermined by white resistance to implementing these decisions and an escalation of violence against blacks.

Despite his stature by this time as one of the most recognized and beloved African American writers, Hughes never emerged as a prominent civil rights leader. It might seem odd, given his commitment to the goals of the movement, that he participated in relatively few demonstrations, read about the March on Washington in a Paris newspaper instead of joining the crowd on the mall, declined an invitation to join Dr. Martin Luther King in Alabama, and, as he cut back on lecturing in the final years of his life, rarely spoke publicly on the issue. It was not on the front lines as a demonstrator, nor even from behind a podium as an orator, that Hughes would make his major contribution to the Freedom Movement, but through his words as a writer.

In the pages of the *Chicago Defender*, Hughes took note of the challenges to Jim Crow posed by various court decisions of the early 1950s. The legal status of segregation was steadily being eroded, and Hughes celebrated these victories while pointing out how far white Americans still had to go to live up to their own professed ideals of democracy and freedom. For example, in a column from December 1952, Hughes wrote about his recent train ride from Jackson, Mississippi, to New Orleans with the writer Melvin Tolson. When he had visited New Orleans two decades earlier, he had been forced to arrive and depart in crowded Jim Crow cars; this time he enjoyed private accommodations on the luxurious Panama Limited, which until recently had not served Negroes at all. Changes in the law forced the company to sell tickets to blacks. Tolson and Hughes had purchased seats in the club car where they would have been seated among the white passengers. Rather than allow them to take their seats, the conductor searched for an unoccupied drawing room where Tolson and Hughes could be segregated from the white passengers, in luxury this time. Hughes mocks the whites for being willing to do "anything to keep the Negroes segregated" even to the extent of giving them superior accommodations at no additional charge. But he concludes on a somber note, observing that despite his luxurious train ride, upon arrival in New Orleans, all black travelers were forced to use the segregated waiting room with no amenities and a filthy restroom ("From Rampart Street" 64–65).

In other columns, sarcastic humor gave way to a sense of outrage at the willingness of white Southerners to accept the persistence of segregation without shame. "I saw [FOR WHITE] signs when I first went South in the 1920s. I still see them there today in 1952. And I haven't yet seen a seen a white Southerner blush" ("Far from Living" 88). He also criticized those blacks who complained that he dwelt on the injustice of segregation too much. "Some Negroes believe that since they have, through wealth, educational or geographical location, managed to avoid the rigors of Jim Crow living, everybody else should have been fortunate or clever enough to have devised such means of escape, too. Well…some folks want the WHOLE U.S.A. to be a decent place racially speaking" ("MacArthur Lives" 63). Hughes urged black writers to keep on protesting the shame and stupidity of Jim Crow laws on a daily basis.

Three events of the mid-1950s brought the obliteration of the Jim Crow car closer by escalating the struggle for civil rights. On May 17, 1954, the Supreme Court ruled in Brown versus the Board of Education that segregated schools and classrooms were unconstitutional. But the white South resisted the implementation of the decision, arguing that their very way of life was at stake. In August 1955, Emmett Till, a young, black teenager from Chicago who was visiting relatives in rural Mississippi, accepted a dare from his friends to flirt with a white woman. When her husband, Roy Bryant, heard of this alleged insult to his wife, he and his half brother J. W. Millam went to Till's uncle's house and forced Emmett to leave with them. They claimed that they had later let the boy go, but he was never seen alive again. Bryant and Millam were arrested on kidnapping charges. A few days later a mutilated body, badly decomposed but identified as Till's by a ring he wore, was found in a local river. The body was transported to Chicago for burial, where it was displayed for three days and viewed by thousands of mourners. Pictures of the body were published in *Jet* magazine. National pressure forced the Mississippi authorities to bring the two men to trial on charges of murder and kidnapping, and even many white Southerners declared their outrage.

However, the men were acquitted after a five-day trial that September. In closing arguments, the defense had appealed to the Anglo-Saxon heritage of the all-white jury and claimed that the trial was really about defending the Southern way of life. Outrage over the killing and the outcome of the trial helped fuel support for the Freedom Movement. The murder of a Northern black boy at the hands of whites made all blacks more aware of their vulnerability. The horror of the case and the further insult of the acquittal led to calls for blacks to register and vote and put pressure on the federal government to enforce its laws against Southern resistance.

The third event took place in December of 1955 when Rosa Parks refused to give up her seat on the bus to a white man. Parks was arrested, but her defiance inspired a 381-day boycott of the public transportation system in Montgomery, Alabama. The boycott was organized by the Montgomery Improvement Association, under the leadership of its president, a young pastor, Dr. Martin Luther King, Jr. Jesse B. Semple, in one of Hughes's columns, declared his admiration for King and suggested he run for President (qtd. in *LLH* II: 264). Hughes would later dedicate his final book, *The Panther and the Lash,* to Rosa Parks, crediting her with "setting off…the boycotts, the sit-ins, the Freedom Rides…" When the city reluctantly voted to comply with a Supreme Court decision declaring segregated buses illegal, the boycott ended with victory for the protestors, but they first endured violence and bombings.

Such hostile responses also accompanied attempts to integrate schools. In 1956, Autherine Lucy enrolled at the University of Alabama, but violent resistance forced her to withdraw. Hughes remarked sarcastically that whites who violently opposed integration in education often had no problem with integration in the bedroom ("A Brickbat for Education" 42). The integration of Central High School in Little Rock, Arkansas, was scheduled for the fall of 1957, but the governor called on the Arkansas National Guard to keep the nine black students who had enrolled from entering the school. Three weeks later, after a court injunction against the governor, the students tried again, only to be stopped by a mob of whites. Finally, President Eisenhower sent paratroopers and other National Guardsmen to force their admission, and the students began attending on September 25, 1957. When one of the students, Ernest Green, graduated the following May, Hughes celebrated his bravery and dedication in a *Chicago Defender* column. In order to earn that diploma, Green had "walked through mobs, endured spit and curses, braved brickbats and passed lines of soldiers with unsure bayonets." Hughes saw in Green's achievement the triumph of a people who persisted in pursuing learning despite "generations of enforced ignorance" ("The Man of the Year" 43–44).

Federal troops had made Green's achievement possible, and Hughes believed that more consistent and overwhelming federal force was needed to force Southerners to comply with the law of the land. Another prominent writer, William Faulkner, felt differently. As Faulkner explained to Du Bois, who challenged him to a debate on integration, he conceded that segregation was wrong "morally, legally and ethically." However, as a practical matter, he counseled "moderation and patience" (Padgett). Du Bois challenged Faulkner in the wake of publicity over a controversial interview that Faulkner gave in February 1956 to the *London Sunday Times*. In the interview, Faulkner was quoted as expressing his determination to defend Mississippi against the aggression of the federal government, even to the point of shooting blacks. Faulkner tried to repudiate the statement in letters to several magazines following the publication of the interview, but made it clear that he opposed federal involvement that would force immediate integration on a reluctant South (Padgett). Hughes was incensed. Writing in the *Chicago Defender* in May 1956, Hughes mocked Faulkner's Nobel Prize acceptance speech of December 1950 in which Faulkner had claimed that "the problems of the human heart in conflict with itself" were the proper subject for literature. Wondering why Faulkner and other Southerners could be so opposed to integration with blacks that they would advocate using violence to defend it, Hughes commented: "He got the Nobel Prize. I thought he loved humanity. But I thought humanity included me." He invited Faulkner to put himself in the place of the colored people before calling on them to be patient, noting that Mississippi had made little discernible racial progress in the more than 90 years since emancipation ("Concerning a Great Mississippi Writer" 91–92). Hughes's animosity toward Faulkner would later prompt him to speak against Faulkner's nomination for the 1962 Gold Medal for Literature awarded by the National Institute of Arts and Letters. Faulkner won anyway and Hughes attended the luncheon where he received the award, expressing his disgust privately in a letter to Arna Bontemps (qtd. in *LLH* II: 352).

Hughes believed that literature could play an important role in furthering the cause of integration. He told a Washington audience in 1958 that "colored literature" could prepare whites to accept integration by helping them to recognize the humanity of blacks and educate both black and white children about the importance of the black contribution "to the struggle and development of America" (qtd. in *LLH* II: 285). To this end, Hughes considered writing a young-adult novel set in the contemporary South and focusing on the civil rights struggle, and accepted a contract to write the history of the NAACP. While his second collection of Simple stories, *Simple Takes a Wife*, had continued in a novelistic vein and focused on Simple's relationship to the various women in his life, Hughes's third collection was a topical book in which Simple offered his views on civil rights. *Simple Stakes a Claim* appeared in the fall of 1957 and was offered as the first selection of the newly formed monthly book club, the Negro Book Society.

In July 1960, Hughes began work on a long poem that would eventually reach 800 lines and be published as the book *Ask Your Mama: Twelve Moods for Jazz*. Hughes drafted the poem repeatedly over the next seven months and finished it in February 1961. The poem consists of a series of 12 mostly free verse sections with occasional rhyming passages. Printed in italics across the page from the verse are musical directions that serve to comment on and amplify the mood of the poem. The poem opens with the music for the "Hesitation Blues," which, according to Hughes's note, functions as the *leitmotif* for the poem. He also included a brief commentary on each section of the poem labeled "liner notes for the poetically unhep." The poem is thick with allusions to black leaders, heroes, writers, and entertainers, and in this allusiveness and its heavy use of annotations and notes can be said to parody *The Waste Land* (and perhaps also Melvin Tolson's 1954 *Libretto for the Republic of Liberia*, which won acclaim from white critics for its deliberately difficult modernist style). Hughes was also consciously playing on the African American tradition of "the dozens," an exchange of ritual insults. Because of its musical aspect, the poem was especially suited to dramatic performance. Soon after Hughes completed the manuscript and before Knopf had accepted it for publication, *Ask Your Mama* was performed on February 6 at the Marketplace Gallery in Harlem with Margaret Bonds at the piano. For a publicity stunt, Hughes had sent invitations to 120 people who were mentioned in the poem including two ardent segregationists. Then he left on a tour that took him to the West Coast and included another performance of *Ask Your Mama*, with a jazz group providing the music, in Santa Monica.

When the poem itself was published in the fall of 1961, it received primarily unfavorable reviews. It was condemned as a weak imitation of Beat poetry, or as a mere novelty that should never have been published. According to Rampersad, Hughes was frustrated that no reviewer recognized his adaptation of the dozens and wrote that he wished he could find "some colored reviewer [to] wake them up" (*LLH* II: 344). But there were some positive reviews. J. Saunders Redding, who had criticized Hughes's last two books of poetry, praised this one, and Rudi Blesh reviewed the book sympathetically in the *New York Herald Tribune*, describing the poem and the expression that gave it its title as "the retort—half derisive, half angry—to the smug, the stupid, the bigoted, the selfish…" Blesh praised Hughes for revealing that the jazz poetry he had been singing for more than 30 years was not merely "'good time' music" but something "bitter yet jubilant," a song of freedom that calls America to task for not offering its freedom to all (41).

In 1962, *Fight for Freedom*, Hughes's history of the NAACP, was published, and Hughes endured an exhausting publicity tour. As the civil rights struggle grew more violent, Hughes felt depressed. He disapproved of black nationalism, and was dismayed by infighting among civil rights groups as to which deserved the most credit. Mostly he was angered by the lack of national progress. In January 1963, he spoke at Wayne State University and declared that the South's intransigence meant that the problem could not be attacked one community at a time. What was needed was a general announcement that integration was inevitable, backed with federal military power (qtd. in *LLH* II:358). Three weeks later at a PEN discussion, Hughes commented sadly on the futility of "relying on the aspirin of a Supreme Court edict when, in some parts of our country, we are suffering the cancer of death" (qtd. in *LLH* II: 359). He also expressed his frustration and bitterness in poems like "Long View: Negro" (*CP* 547–48), "Sweet Words on Race" (*CP* 560), and "Go Slow" (*CP* 537–38):

> Go slow, they say—
> While the bite
> Of the dog is fast.
> Go slow, I hear—
> While they tell me
> You can't eat here!
> You can't live here!
> You can't work here!
> Don't demonstrate! Wait!—
> While they lock the gate. (1–10)

The summer of 1963 was one of rising violence as a result of the civil rights movement, and, conscious of criticism of the political irrelevance of his *Tambourines to Glory*, a musical comedy about a Harlem storefront church then in production for a Broadway appearance, Hughes began to draft a new gospel play that would take the freedom movement for its theme. He called the new play *Jericho-Jim Crow*.

As *Tambourines to Glory* prepared to go into rehearsals, Hughes left for a grand tour of Europe. He was in Paris during the celebrated March on Washington where Martin Luther King delivered his powerful "I Have a Dream" speech. Soon after his return, Hughes was approached by producer Joel Schenker who had concerns about the forthcoming production of *Tambourines to Glory*. At such an exciting time in black America, when everyone was still uplifted by the March on Washington, wouldn't their production risk charges of frivolity? Why not add a brief scene to the script in which a character would speak on behalf of the civil rights struggle? Hughes refused because he saw *Tambourines to Glory* as an apolitical play, an entertaining drama of black life that might attract an audience tired of racial controversy.

The play opened at New York's Little Theater on 44th Street in November 1963. Reviewers lambasted the play for being inadequately rehearsed and for unevenly blending comedy, drama, satire, and music. Furthermore Hughes was criticized for presenting a distorted and negative picture of the black church at a time when it was playing a significant role in the civil rights struggle. The show closed in only three weeks, having lost $125,000 (*LLH* II: 370).

With *Jericho-Jim Crow*, Hughes took care to avoid the mistakes of *Tambourines to Glory*. For its producer, he chose Stella Holt, who had successfully produced *Black Nativity* for Hughes a few years earlier, and aimed for a low-budget production in Greenwich Village at the Sanctuary, a church with a theater in its basement. The theme of the play was political, and Hughes reinforced its message by designating a benefit performance with the proceeds to be divided between the Congress of Racial Equality, the Student Non-Violent Coordinating Committee, and the NAACP. He also decided that nonprofit groups that used any funds raised to support the Freedom Movement would be allowed to stage the play without paying any royalties. He even had a group of ministers visit a rehearsal to certify that black religion was portrayed respectfully.

Jericho-Jim Crow was a stunning critical success and did much to erase the pain of the failure of *Tambourines to Glory*. The play ran through the end of April. Then, rather than going to Broadway, the play toured other theaters in the surrounding metropolitan area. It continued to be popular, but critical attention turned to a much more shocking play, Le Roi Jones's *Dutchman*, which tells of a white woman who taunts, flirts with, and finally murders a young black man on the subway. Though disturbed by the profanity in Jones's play, Hughes could not deny the power of what he dubbed "a battering ram treatment of the race problem" (qtd. in *LLH* II: 376).

While *Jericho-Jim Crow* demonstrated his commitment to the cause of the Freedom Movement, some of Hughes's publications in the early sixties seemed to put him out of step with the more radical mood of younger black writers. For example, the two volumes of his autobiography were reissued by Hill and Wang in 1961 and 1963, respectively. One reviewer of this new edition of *The Big Sea* accused Hughes of suppressing his racial self, failing to communicate to the reader a sense of his blackness (qtd. in *LLH* II: 376). The *Book of Negro Humor*, based on an old manuscript, was eventually published by Dodd, Mead in 1966, but was rejected earlier by Indiana University Press on the grounds that the humor was outdated and often at the expense of black dignity. And when the anthology *New Negro Poets, USA* was published in 1964 by Indiana University Press, it was criticized for presenting poems that failed to engage the important racial questions now facing the nation.

In July 1964, riots erupted in Harlem, touched off by the shooting of a black youth by a white policeman. The unrest escalated as Harlem residents threw bottles at white policemen and firebombed businesses. Hughes could hear gunfire from his home. Although only one person was killed in the riots, 140 were hurt, and hundreds were arrested.

Hughes was deeply agitated by these events. He participated in a television broadcast on CBS where he urged calm, but he wrote bitterly about the inevitability of violent black response in the face of continued racism in the *New York Post* (for which he had begun writing a weekly column in 1962, when his relationship with the *Defender* was under strain because of tardy payment for his work). He also wrote the poem "Death in Yorkville" which both laments the reality of "100 years NOT free" and honors the resilience of the black spirit that is "still alive" after decades of brutality (*CP* 554–55).

Disturbed by the riot, Hughes was also troubled by the more radical approach of emerging leaders like Malcolm X and Stokely Carmichael. A column in the *New York Post* questioned the tactics of writers like Le Roi Jones who sought to shock with offensive language and of leaders who argued for black separatism (qtd. in *LLH* II: 383). When Malcolm X was murdered in February 1965, and whips, clubs and tear gas were used against Martin Luther King and 500 marchers in Selma, Alabama, Hughes was horrified. When President Johnson spoke in favor of the Civil Rights Act, Hughes sent an approving telegram. But when Martin Luther

King telegraphed Hughes inviting him to join a second march from Selma to Montgomery, Hughes did not accept. Instead, he continued to speak through his writing.

In *Simple's Uncle Sam*, published in 1965, Hughes allows Boyd to express the hope he still cherishes that racial progress is inevitable, while Simple expresses his bitterness, cynicism, and frustration, despite the humorous tone of many of the exchanges. Boyd advocates nonviolence, but Simple notes that since violence has worked well enough to discourage blacks from voting and to keep them out of schools, perhaps it will work as well against the whites if all the blacks were to join forces and "rise up in one mass" to demand their rights (119). When Boyd tries to assure Simple that "segregation will end and the ballot will come in due time," Simple counters, "So will death" (177). The book also includes an adaptation of part of the "Cultural Exchange" sequence of *Ask Your Mama*. Simple recounts his dream of a world where blacks live in mansions and speak patronizingly to their loyal white retainers. But Simple awakens "to the same old nightmare" (132).

Hughes did not live to see the end of the nightmare. He witnessed the passage of the Voting Rights Act of 1965 but he died before the assassination of Dr. King, the riots that followed, the battles over busing and school desegregation, and the advent of affirmative action. His final collection, *The Panther and the Lash*, which he prepared for publication just before his death, offered both new and old poems reflecting on the struggle for justice and racial equality. As one reviewer remarked, "It is indeed fitting that the volume with which his career ended is a vital contribution to [the civil rights movement] as well as to American poetry" (Farrison 44).

Chapter 21

HUGHES'S FINAL YEARS

In the last two decades of his life, Hughes not only continued his work as a poet, playwright, lyricist, and journalist, but worked in other genres as well. He collaborated with photographer Roy DeCarava on *the Sweet Fly-paper of Life* (1955), writing text for the young photographer's series of photos of Harlem life. He worked with Milton Meltzer on *A Pictorial History of Negro Life*, wrote liner notes for numerous albums, and published several nonfiction books for young readers. Despite his quarrels with Meyerowitz over his tendency to write a score that drowned out the lyrics, Hughes continued to collaborate with him, producing several librettos including the opera *Esther* and the Easter cantata, *The Glory around His Head*. He published a total of five collections featuring Jesse B. Semple between 1950 and 1965 and developed the second book, *Simple Takes a Wife*, into both a straight play and a musical, *Simply Heavenly*. He wrote five Gospel plays—*Black Nativity, Tambourines to Glory, Jericho-Jim Crow, The Prodigal Son,* and *The Gospel Glory*—and also published *Tambourines to Glory* as a novel in 1958. He devoted his literary talents to the cause of African independence as well as to civil rights, resumed international travel, and even represented the U.S. State Department. While in the early 1950s he struggled financially, referred to himself as a "literary share-cropper" who churned out books and articles for scant profit (Nichols 277), and worried over his declining status in relation to younger writers, by the time of his death he was enjoying renewed popularity and respect and had been the recipient of numerous awards and honors.

Hughes had long been generous in his encouragement of younger writers. In the final years of his life he continued these efforts, with special attention to the work of young African writers. He was also proud to witness the success of some of his protégés, delighting, for instance, in the selection of Gwendolyn Brooks as the winner of the Pulitzer Prize for poetry in 1950 for her book *Annie Allen*. But about others' success he had mixed feelings, especially that of James Baldwin, who not only wrote in ways Hughes did not quite approve of, but who also spoke critically or dismissively of Hughes's work, and of Ralph Ellison and Melvin Tolson, who received favorable attention from white critics who had never taken Hughes as seriously.

Hughes had jumped from Knopf to Henry Holt with the publication of *Montage of a Dream Deferred* in 1951. Though Hughes had been very enthusiastic about the book, it did not receive the strong critical response he had hoped it would evoke. J. Saunders Redding claimed that the work was stale, focused on the same old emotions and experiences. In the *New York Times*, Babette Deutsch reviewed it as an example of "the limitations of folk art," and dismissed Hughes's repeated use of the word "dream" as sentimentality (32) though several observers would note echoes of some of Hughes's poems in King's famous "I Have a Dream" speech 12 years later (*LLH* II: 367).

His second publication with Holt was a collection of short stories, most of which had been published before in magazines and some of which dated back to the 1930s. Called *Laughing to Keep from Crying*, it lacked the unity of *The Ways of White Folks* and the most common response of reviewers was that the quality of the stories was uneven. The book was soon eclipsed anyway by attention to Ralph Ellison's long-awaited novel, *Invisible Man*. Hughes viewed Ellison as something of a protégé, and had dedicated *Montage of a Dream Deferred* to him and his wife. But by this time Ellison was less than enthusiastic about Hughes's work. Indeed, he had been insulted several years earlier when Hughes failed to offer any feedback on some material Ellison had sent him from his novel in progress, but had then suggested that Ellison might want a job turning the Simple columns into a book. In Ellison's judgment, Hughes had become rather frivolous. Hughes praised *Invisible Man* in print but admitted in a letter to a friend in 1953 that he had not yet finished the book (qtd. in *LLH* II 201).

Hughes had much greater reservations about the work of James Baldwin. In February 1953, Hughes's former publisher, Knopf, brought out Baldwin's novel *Go Tell It on the Mountain*. Privately, Hughes strongly disliked the novel, which he thought strove too hard to be literary (Nichols 302), and, like much recent writing by young blacks that he had criticized in an essay for *Harlem Quarterly*, was tainted by excessive use of violence, profanity, and graphic sexuality (*LLH* II: 207). He was also hurt by an essay by Richard Gibson in the magazine *Perspectives*, which advised young black writers to view themselves as contemporaries of writers like Joyce, Kafka, Eliot, and Pound "and not merely of Langston Hughes" (qtd. in *LLH* II: 206).

Hughes felt that Baldwin, like Richard Wright before him, had estranged himself from the black race by going to live abroad, and that he tried too hard to be intellectual. Baldwin wrote novels that did not feature black characters and he depicted Harlem unfavorably. On the other hand, Hughes's own focus on racial consciousness and his celebration of black difference seemed to some young writers to be out of date in an age of integration. In 1956, Hughes had occasion to review Baldwin's essay collection *Notes of a Native Son* in the *New York Times* and though he praised Baldwin's strengths, he depicted him as a still-maturing writer who had not yet reached his true potential. Baldwin had his turn when he reviewed Hughes's *Selected Poems* in the same paper in 1959. Baldwin accused Hughes of failing to accomplish much despite his considerable talents, and of including poems in the collection that should have been discarded (37–38).

In 1954, Hughes was also somewhat dismayed to learn that the poet Melvin Tolson was suddenly being acclaimed by the white establishment. Tolson, who wrote in a modernist style, was praised for displaying command of the "language of the Anglo-American tradition," while paradoxically also being portrayed by critics such as Allen Tate as offering a more authentic "Negro quality" than poets like Brooks or Hughes (qtd. in *LLH* II: 235). Tate wrote this as an introduction to Tolson's *Libretto for the Republic of Liberia*. The poem was deliberately difficult, full of obscure allusions, and seemed to Hughes to win the attention of white critics for that reason. As discussed in the previous chapter, the allusive style and use of footnotes in *Ask Your Mama* may partly have been conceived as a reply to Tolson. Where Tolson used "foreign words and footnotes" to win the respect of white critics—as Hughes observed in a letter to Bontemps (Nichols 390)—Hughes's allusions were to black culture, aimed not at white academics but African American readers.

Around the same time that Hughes began to feel that he was losing ground to younger black writers on the American literary scene, he accepted an invitation to judge the annual short story contest of *Drum: Africa's Leading Magazine*. This experience renewed his interest in Africa and made him determined to bring African voices to the attention of American readers. Without encouragement from any publisher, he solicited short stories from all the young African writers whose names came to his attention. After a year of work he had assembled two collections.

But neither was ever accepted by a publisher despite dedicated efforts to circulate them. Undaunted, though the work was costly both in terms of time and money, Hughes continued his efforts. He also took a strong interest in the rise of independent African nations. For instance, he supported the newly independent African nation of Ghana and was one of the leaders of a drive to collect donations of books and art to send to the young country. By the late 1950s, he was able to find publishers interested in African work, and began to assemble a new collection. In 1960, Crown published his anthology *An African Treasury: Articles, Essays, Stories, and Poems by Black Africans*.

Another tie to Africa came in the form of an adopted son. After reading one of Hughes's poems that had been reprinted in an African literary magazine, a Nigerian teenager named Chuba Nweke wrote an admiring letter to Hughes. Claiming that the poem had inspired him to finish a short story and five poems, Nweke enclosed the story and asked for Hughes's guidance. He signed his letter, "your son, Chuba Nweke." Touched, Hughes replied warmly, offering general encouragement rather than specific praise and asking Nweke to send a photograph. Nweke eagerly complied but after awhile Hughes found keeping up with his "son's" demanding correspondence too much, and replied only infrequently.

By the late 1950s Hughes found himself in demand as a lecturer and was able to raise his fees. He recorded some of his poems for the Library of Congress. Featured in a 1958 *Life* magazine story as "one of the blacks who brought honor to the United States" (qtd. in *LLH* II: 285), Hughes could not resist commenting on the difference between this story and the one that had labeled him a communist dupe in 1949. Many of Hughes's recent works were being translated into other languages including Czech, Hindi, French, Portuguese, Arabic, and Japanese. These included his children's books *Famous American Negroes* and *The First Book of Jazz*, his Simple volumes, excerpts from his autobiographies, and selections from his poetry.

With his *Selected Poems* scheduled to appear from Knopf in 1959, Hughes discreetly began to solicit his own nomination for that year's Spingarn Medal by sending a list of his achievements and a packet of publicity material to friends whom he believed might nominate him. To Hughes, his literary achievements and his having supported himself exclusively as a writer since about 1925 were strong reasons to support his nomination in the year his selected works were published (Nichols 375–76). The Spingarn Medal was given annually by the NAACP to a black American on the basis of high achievement in any field. But Hughes was disappointed. The award for 1959 went to Duke Ellington.

However, in the summer of the following year, Hughes was informed that he had won the Spingarn Medal for 1960. He attended the NAACP convention to accept his award. Speaking of the importance of black folk culture to his art and his overriding concern to present the lives and dignity of black Americans in his work, he accepted his award "in the name of Negro people who have given me the materials out of which my poems and stories, plays and songs have come from...as well as their love, understanding, and support." He urged young Negro writers not to be afraid to write about their own lives ("Langston Hughes's Acceptance of the Spingarn Medal").

Throughout the 1960s Hughes seized several opportunities for international travel and often had the opportunity to attend foreign productions of his plays. He traveled to Trinidad in November 1959 to give a series of lectures and there had a chance to meet Anne Marie Coussey Wooding, whom Hughes had once courted in Paris. Now married with several grown children, she congratulated Hughes on his success and reminisced with him about their Paris days. Hughes gave four talks focusing on both race relations and on poetry by black Americans. He met various political leaders involved in the progress of the British West Indies toward independence.

Next, Africa beckoned Hughes again after an absence of nearly 40 years. Hughes traveled to Nigeria at the end of 1960 at the invitation of Nnamadi Azikiwe, who was to be inaugurated as the chief executive of the newly independent nation. Azikiwe, a former classmate at Lincoln University, had charted a plane to take his American guests to his inaugural ceremonies. He closed his inaugural address by reciting one of Hughes's poems from *The Weary Blues*. Hughes finally met Chuba Nweke on this trip, but the two did not establish a close relationship. Nweke would soon be supplanted in Hughes's affections by another young Nigerian, Sunday Osuya. Osuya was the policeman assigned to keep the crowds away from the visiting dignitaries. Impressed by his polite and efficient work, Hughes asked for his name and address and promised to write to him.

During the Christmas season of 1961, Hughes returned to Nigeria to participate in a festival as part of a delegation of performers organized by the American Society of African Cultures. Hughes was the master of ceremonies at one of two major concerts arranged as part of the festival. He spent over a month in Nigeria traveling and visiting with Osuya, whom he also met on a third visit to Africa six months later.

In June 1962, he attended a writers' conference at a university in Uganda and also spoke at the dedication of a U.S. Information Service center and library in Ghana. Hughes was made the guest of honor at the conference. Before returning home he visited Egypt, Rome, and finally Spoleto, Italy, where *Black Nativity* was being performed at a folk festival. The production was so well received at the festival that a European tour followed. Later it would have a successful week of performances at Lincoln Center.

Back at home Hughes was often asked by the State Department to play host to various foreign visitors who were interested in Harlem, especially writers. He found himself invited to numerous dinner parties and receptions, social obligations that he grumbled about but also enjoyed. In November of 1961, he attended a dinner at the White House during the visit of Léopold Sédar Senghor, the president of Senegal. A poet himself, Senghor had suggested inviting Hughes and publicly toasted him as a major influence on his own work during the dinner.

This was not his last visit to the White House. In October 1962, he went to Washington, D.C. for the first national poetry festival. He served on the panel "The Poet and the Public" and attended a White House reception. One of the more dynamic readers, he received a standing ovation. Other awards and honors for Hughes included an honorary doctorate from Howard University in 1963 and election to the National Institute of Arts and Letters in 1961.

In the spring of 1965, he toured Europe giving a series of lectures on African American writing and readings of his work. The State Department allowed him to select other writers to accompany him, and true to his habit of supporting and encouraging younger talents, he selected Paule Marshall and William M. Kelley. The tour was exhausting but gratifying. It would be his last trip abroad though he was contemplating an extended trip to Paris at the time of his death.

On May 6, 1967, Langston Hughes appeared at the emergency room of the New York Polyclinic Hospital reporting severe abdominal pain. Registering under the name of James L. Hughes, he may have wanted to remain anonymous. According to Rampersad, Raoul Abdul, who had worked as Hughes's secretary intermittently since 1958, disputes Faith Berry's contention that Hughes was viewed as an indigent patient, and left untreated until an orderly recognized him as the famous poet (Berry 328). Hospital records indicate that treatment began upon admission. Hughes was diagnosed with an enlarged and possibly cancerous prostate. Although a biopsy proved negative, surgery was scheduled for May 12 to remove the enlarged gland (*LLH* II: 421). Although he survived the operation, he soon began showing signs of infection and died on May 22 of septic shock due to bacteria entering his bloodstream as a result of the surgery.

A memorial service was arranged for May 25 at a Harlem funeral home. Following for the most part Hughes's playful instructions that the service was to consist entirely of music, George Bass arranged for the jazz pianist Randy Weston to entertain. Together with a drummer and bass player, Weston played several jazz or blues numbers, then Arna Bontemps spoke briefly and read some of Hughes's poems. The funeral ended as Hughes had requested, with the number "Do Nothing 'Til You Hear from Me." Later that day just before Hughes was cremated, a smaller group of mourners solemnly recited the lyrics of Hughes's first great poem, "The Negro Speaks of Rivers." With those words and the many that were to follow, he had touched their lives and the lives of his many readers, both black and white.

ABBREVIATIONS
FOR TEXTS CITED

BS   Hughes, Langston. *The Big Sea*. New York: Knopf, 1940; Hill and Wang, 1993.

CP   Hughes, Langston. *The Collected Poems of Langston Hughes*, Ed. Arnold Rampersad and David Roessel. New York: Vintage, 1994.

IW   Hughes, Langston. *I Wonder as I Wander*. New York: Rinehart, 1956; Hill and Wang, 1993.

LLH   Rampersad, Arnold. *The Life of Langston Hughes*, 2nd ed. 2 vols. New York: Oxford UP, 2002.

MB   Bass, George Houston and Henry Louis Gates, Jr., eds. *Mule Bone: A Comedy of Negro Life: Edited with Introductions by George Houston Bass and Henry Louis Gates, Jr. and the Complete Story of the* Mule Bone *Controversy*. New York: Harper Perennial, 1991.

SELECTED BIBLIOGRAPHY

WORKS CITED

Anderson, Sherwood. "Paying for Old Sins." *The Nation* 11 July 1934: 49–50. Rpt. in Mullen 64–66.

Baldwin, James. Rev. of *Selected Poems*. *New York Times Book Review* 29 Mar. 1959: 6. Rpt. in Gates and Appiah 37–38.

Bass, George Houston, and Henry Louis Gates, Jr., eds. *Mule Bone: A Comedy of Negro Life: Edited with Introductions by George Houston Bass and Henry Louis Gates, Jr. and the Complete Story of the* Mule Bone *Controversy*. New York: Harper Perennial, 1991.

Bernard, Emily, ed. *Remember Me to Harlem: The Letters of Langston Hughes and Carl Van Vechten, 1924–1964*. New York: Knopf, 2001.

Berry, Faith. *Langston Hughes: Before and Beyond Harlem*. Westport, Conn.: Lawrence Hill, 1983.

Blesh, Rudi. Rev. of *Ask Your Mama*. *New York Herald Tribune* 26 Nov. 1961. Rpt. in Gates and Appiah 41.

Bontemps, Arna. "The Awakening: A Memoir." *The Harlem Renaissance Remembered*. New York: Dodd, Mead, 1972. 1–26.

"Closing Testimony of Langston Hughes before the Senate Committee on Permanent Investigations." 26 Mar. 1953. 2 pp. JWJ MSS 26, Box 365, Folder 5863.

"Copy of Transcript." State Department Information Program. Senate Permanent Subcommittee on Investigations of the Subcommittee on Operations." 8 pp. JWJ MSS 26, Box 365, Folder 5862.

Daniel, Walter C. "Langston Hughes versus the Black Preachers in the *Pittsburgh Courier* in the 1930s." Mullen 129–35.

De Santis, Christopher C., ed. *Langston Hughes and the* Chicago Defender: *Essays on Race, Politics and Culture, 1942–1962.* Urbana: U of Illinois P, 1995.

Deutsch, Babette. "Waste Land of Harlem." *New York Times Book Review* 6 May 1951: 23. Rpt. in Gates and Appiah 32.

Duffy, Susan. *The Political Plays of Langston Hughes.* Carbondale: Southern Illinois UP, 2000.

Farrison, W. Edward. Rev. of *The Panther and the Lash. College Language Association Journal* March 1968. Rpt. in Gates and Appiah 42–44.

Gates, Henry Louis, Jr. "A Tragedy of Negro Life." Bass and Gates 5–24.

Gates, Henry Louis, Jr., and K. A. Appiah, eds. *Langston Hughes: Critical Perspectives Past and Present.* New York: Amistad, 1993.

Hemenway, Robert E. "Excerpt from *Zora Neale Hurston: A Literary Biography.*" Bass and Gates 161–89.

Hughes, Langston. "The Accusers' Names Nobody Will Remember, but History Records Du Bois." *Chicago Defender* 6 Oct. 1951. Rpt. in De Santis 187–88.

———. *The Big Sea.* New York: Knopf, 1940. Hill and Wang, 1993.

———. "A Brickbat for Education—A Kiss for the Bedroom in Dixie." *Chicago Defender* 24 Mar. 1956. Rpt. in De Santis 40–41.

———. "Concerning a Great Mississippi Writer and the Southern Negro." *Chicago Defender* 26 May 1956. Rpt. in De Santis 91–92.

———. *The Collected Poems of Langston Hughes.* Ed. Arnold Rampersad and David Roessel. New York: Vintage, 1994.

———. "The Fall of Berlin." *Chicago Defender* 12 May 1945. Rpt. in De Santis 135–37.

———. "Far from Living Up to Its Name, Dixie Has Neither Manners Nor Shame." *Chicago Defender* 26 Apr. 1952. Rpt. in De Santis 87–89.

———. "From Rampart Street to Harlem, I Follow the Trail of the Blues." *Chicago Defender* 6 Dec. 1952. Rpt. in De Santis 64–65.

———. *I Wonder as I Wander.* New York: Rinehart, 1956. Hill and Wang, 1993.

———. "Langston Hughes' Acceptance of the Spingarn Medal." 26 June, 1960. NAACP Convention, St. Paul, MN. JWJ MSS 26, Box 482, Folder 12182.

———. "MacArthur Lives in the Waldorf-Astoria; Gilbert Lives in Jail." *Chicago Defender* 2 June 1951. Rpt. in De Santis 62–63.

———. "The Man of the Year for 1958." *Chicago Defender* 14 June 1958. Rpt. in De Santis 43–44.

———. "My America." *The Langston Hughes Reader.* New York: Braziller, 1958: 500–501.

———. "The Negro Artist and the Racial Mountain." *The Nation* 23 June 1926. <http://past.thenation.com/historic/bhm2000/19260223hughes.shtml>.

———. *Not Without Laughter*. New York: Knopf, 1930.

———. "A Portent and a Warning to the Negro People from Hughes." *Chicago Defender* 5 Feb. 1949. Rpt. in De Santis 184–85.

———. "Statement in Round Numbers Concerning the Relative Merits of 'Way Down South' and 'Don't You Want to Be Free?' As Complied by the Author Mr. Langston Hughes." JWJ MSS 26, Box 367, Folder 5927.

———. "Statement to the Senate Permanent Subcommittee on Investigations." 23 Mar. 1953. JWJ MSS 26, Box 365, Folder 5862.

———. *The Ways of White Folks*. New York: Knopf, 1934. Vintage, 1990.

Hutchinson, George. *The Harlem Renaissance in Black and White*. Cambridge, Mass.: Harvard UP, 1995.

JWJ MSS 26, Langston Hughes Collection. Yale Collection of American Literature, Beinecke Rare Book and Manuscript Library.

Kramer, Victor A., and Robert A. Russ, eds. *Harlem Renaissance Re-Examined: A Revised and Expanded Edition*. Troy, NY: Whitson, 1997.

Locke, Alain. Rev. of *The Ways of White Folks*. *Survey Graphic* 23 (1934): 565. Rpt. in Mullen 66–67.

Mullen, Edward J. *Critical Essays on Langston Hughes*. Boston: G.K. Hall, 1986.

Nichols, Charles H., ed. *Arna Bontemps—Langston Hughes Letters: 1925–1967*. New York: Dodd, Mead 1980.

Pacheco, Patrick. " A Discovery Worth the Wait." Rev. of *Mule Bone* by Zora Neale Hurston and Langston Hughes. Lincoln Center Theater, New York. *Los Angeles Times* 24 Feb. 1991: 4.

Padgett, John B. "William Faulkner." *The Mississippi Writers' Page*. 24 Jan. 2002. <http://www.olemiss.edu/depts/english/ms-writers/dir/faulkner_ william/>.

Rampersad, Arnold. *The Life of Langston Hughes*. 2nd ed. 2 vols. New York: Oxford UP, 2002.

Redding, J. Saunders. "Old Form, Old Rhythms, New Worlds." *Saturday Review of Literature* 22 Jan. 1949: 24. Rpt. in Mullen 73–74.

Rich, Frank. "A Difficult Birth for *Mule Bone*." Rev. of *Mule Bone* by Zora Neale Hurston and Langston Hughes. Lincoln Center Theater, New York. *New York Times* 15 Feb. 1991: 1.

Schuyler, George. "Negro-Art Hokum." *The Nation* 16 June 1926. <http://past. thenation.com/historic/bhm2000/19260216schuyler.shtml>.

Story, Ralph D. "Gender and Ambition: Zora Neale Hurston in the Harlem Renaissance." *The Black Scholar* 20.2 (1989): 25–31. Rpt. in *Critical Essays on Zora Neale Hurston*. Ed. Gloria L. Cronin. New York: G.K. Hall, 1998.

SELECTED BOOKS BY LANGSTON HUGHES

Poetry

The Weary Blues. New York: Knopf, 1926.
Fine Clothes to the Jew. New York: Knopf, 1927.
The Dream Keeper and Other Poems. New York: Knopf, 1932.
Shakespeare in Harlem. New York: Knopf, 1942.
Fields of Wonder. New York: Knopf, 1947.
One-Way Ticket. New York: Knopf, 1949.
Montage of a Dream Deferred. New York: Holt, 1951.
Selected Poems. New York: Knopf, 1959.
Ask Your Mama: 12 Moods for Jazz. New York: Knopf, 1961.
The Panther and the Lash: Poems of Our Times. New York: Knopf, 1967.

Prose

Not Without Laughter. New York: Knopf, 1930.
The Ways of White Folks. New York: Knopf, 1934.
The Big Sea. New York: Knopf, 1940.
Simple Speaks His Mind. New York: Simon and Schuster, 1950.
Laughing to Keep from Crying. New York: Holt, 1952.
Simple Takes a Wife. New York: Simon and Schuster, 1953.
I Wonder as I Wander. New York: Rinehart, 1956.
Simple Stakes a Claim. New York: Rinehart, 1957
Tambourines to Glory. New York: John Day, 1958.
The Best of Simple. New York: Hill and Wang, 1961.
Something in Common and Other Stories. New York: Hill and Wang, 1963.
Simple's Uncle Sam. New York: Hill and Wang, 1965.

Drama

Five Plays. Ed. and Introd. Webster Smalley. Bloomington: Indiana UP, 1963.
The Political Plays of Langston Hughes with Introductions and Analyses by Susan Duffy. Carbondale: Southern Illinois UP, 2000.

RECOMMENDED READING

Barksdale, Richard. *Langston Hughes. The Poet and His Critics*. Chicago: American Library Association, 1977.

Bloom, Harold, ed. *Langston Hughes. Modern Critical Views*. New York: Chelsea House, 1989.

Daniel, Cecilia C. A *Centennial Tribute to Langston Hughes*. Feb. 2002. Howard University Library. <http://www.founders.howard.edu/reference/Langston_Hughes2.htm>.

Dawahare, Anthony. "Langston Hughes's Radical Poetry and the 'End of Race.'" MELUS 21 (1998): 21–41.

Ford, Karen Jackson. "Do Right to Write Right: Langston Hughes's Aesthetics of Simplicity." *Twentieth Century Literature* 38.4 (1992): 436–57.

Harper, Donna Sullivan. *Not So Simple: The Simple Stories by Langston Hughes*. Columbia: U of Missouri P, 1995.

Kamsler, Christopher. *The Langston Hughes Tribute Site*. 11 Sept. 1999. <http://www.langstonhughes.8m.com/>.

Komunyakaa, Yusef. "Langston Hughes + Poetry = The Blues." *Callaloo* 25 (2002): 1140–43.

Lowney, John. "Langston Hughes and the 'Nonsense' of BeBop." *American Literature* 72 (2000): 357–85.

Manuel, Carme. "*Mule Bone*: Langston Hughes and Zora Neale Hurston's Dream Deferred of an African American Theater of the Black Word." *African American Review* 35 (2001):77–92.

Michlin, Monica. "Langston Hughes's Blues." *Temples for Tomorrow: Looking Back at the Harlem Renaissance*. Ed. Geneviève Fabre and Michel Feith. Bloomington: Indiana UP, 2001 236–58.

Onwuchweka, Jemie. *Langston Hughes: An Introduction to the Poetry*. New York: Columbia UP, 1976.

Sundquist, Eric J. "Who Was Langston Hughes?" *Commentary* December 1996: 55–61.

Tracy, Steven C. "Blues to Live By: Langston Hughes's 'The Blues I'm Playing.'" *Langston Hughes Review* 12.1 (1993): 12–18.

———. *Langston Hughes and the Blues*. Urbana: U of Illinois P, 1988.

Vendler, Helen. "The Unweary Blues." *New Republic* 6 Mar. 1995: 37–42.

INDEX

About the Author

LAURIE F. LEACH is Associate Professor of English at Hawaii Pacific University.